"*A*n organization that ministers to hurting women throughout the world, we have found only a handful of pastors and churches who consider ministry to these families a mission field just as vital as mission work overseas. I consider Don Stewart to be a missionary who is offering hope to hurting women and children. He gives practical advice to those who can't see their way out of an abusive relationship and presents a much-needed wake-up call to the Christian community to get as involved in saving lives as they are in saving souls. It is a privilege to recommend this outstanding book and to celebrate Don Stewart's tireless efforts in helping women find refuge out of domestic violence and abuse."

—*Brenda Branson*
president, FOCUS Ministries, Inc.
Focusministries1.org

Refuge

A Pathway Out
of Domestic
Violence and Abuse

DETECTIVE SERGEANT DONALD STEWART

new
hope
PUBLISHERS

Birmingham, Alabama

New Hope® Publishers
P. O. Box 12065
Birmingham, AL 35202-2065
www.newhopepubl.com

Library of Congress Cataloging-in-Publication Data
Stewart, Donald, Detective Sergeant.
Refuge : a pathway out of domestic violence and abuse / Donald
Stewart.
p. cm.
ISBN 1-56309-811-3 (softcover)
1. Church work with problem families. 2. Family violence-Religious
aspects-Christianity. I. Title.
BV4438.5.S74 2004
261.8'327—dc22
2003022860

ISBN: 1-56309-811-3

N044105 • 0304 • 7.5M1

Dedication

This book is dedicated to the domestic violence advocates, police officers, prosecutors, judges, doctors, nurses, pastors, counselors, and mental health professionals who labor daily to provide food, shelter, safety, justice, healing, and hope to women and children victims of domestic violence.

Never lose heart,
never give up—Win!

Don Stewart

Table of Contents

FOREWORD BY JAN SILVIOUS 11

ACKNOWLEDGMENTS 15

INTRODUCTION. 17

CHAPTER ONE:
**Family Violence and Betrayal
from the Beginning** 21

CHAPTER TWO:
Profile of the Abuser 33

CHAPTER THREE:
Profile of the Abused 57

CHAPTER FOUR:
The Effects of Domestic Violence on Children 69

CHAPTER FIVE:
Understanding Your Worth as a Woman 79

CHAPTER SIX:
**Cowards in the Kingdom: Case Histories of
Domestic Violence** 97

CHAPTER SEVEN:

Our Judicial System: What You Need to Know
and Expect. 105

CHAPTER EIGHT:

Escaping the Wrath of Your Abuser 139

CHAPTER NINE:

Jesus, Victor Over Violence 155

CHAPTER TEN:

Triumph Over Tragedy. 173

CHAPTER ELEVEN:

Ministering to the Abused: Instructions
to Pastors and Those Who Counsel 195

CHAPTER TWELVE:

The Role and Responsibility of the Church
in Ministering to the Abuser 207

CHAPTER THIRTEEN:

Starting Over: Getting Your Life Back on Track . . . 221

APPENDIX A 234

Foreword
by Jan Silvious

Abuse and *violence* are such ugly words. They smack of pain and all kinds of dysfunction. Add the word *domestic* to them and you have words that just should not fit together, yet tragically they do. How on earth can the word that means (according to Webster's) "devoted to home duties and pleasures" be combined with "injury to something that deserves respect?" In the mind of a rational person, *domestic* and *violence* should never be used together, and yet in our country an act of domestic violence occurs every 12 seconds. That is a frightening statistic that is hard to get our minds around. We don't know what to do with such a horrific fact, and we don't know what to do about it.

Many of us have lived in denial a long time. We have convinced ourselves that abuse is something we read about in the newspaper or glimpse on the evening news. It happens to people in bad living conditions, to old people who have no defense, and to little children and animals who are easy to pick on, but what on earth can any of us do about these isolated incidents? Isn't that why we have the police? Isn't that why we have societies for the protection of elders, children, and animals? Don't we have shelters? Don't we have ways to curb abuse and make it go away? Unfortunately, abuse isn't confined to a few dramatic cases you read about from time to time.

Abuse is happening behind closed doors all over this country, and it is not just in low-income housing or in ill-run nursing homes or houses where crackheads keep little babies in fly-infested cribs. Abuse is happening in respectable neighborhoods and upper-income homes. Because abuse and violence emanate from a deceitful heart, it will be found wherever there are unregenerate people. From trailer homes to penthouses, from mansions to mud huts, abuse happens and families are left with scars.

Detective Sergeant Donald Stewart has written a classic work that will open your eyes to the raw reality of abuse. During his 25 years as a policeman, he lived on the front lines dealing with domestic violence. He has seen murder, sexual assault, beatings, hostage taking, stalking, and harassment. It would be no exaggeration to say that Don Stewart has seen it all. As a result, and with a passion that only comes from firsthand experience, Don has thoughtfully compiled a work of depth, sophistication, and insight, one which every thinking adult needs to read. With the competence and confidence of a veteran policeman, he gives the layperson facts and findings that will open your eyes, and offers answers for the harsh questions that inevitably arise when a woman or a child is being abused.

I first met Don Stewart several years ago when he was a guest on a national Christian call-in program called Precept Live. I was a co-host on the program and our topic for the evening was domestic abuse. As caller after caller phoned in, I was warmed and impressed with Detective Sergeant Stewart's straightforward, compassionate answers. Here was a Christian law officer who was not afraid to offer help and counsel to women who found themselves in grave danger or ongoing distress. With a clear head and wise counsel, Don offered help and hope in a very personable, definitive way. He never hedged with weak, impractical answers. Because he was so well received and we were so impressed with his ability to see the problem clearly and to offer truly significant help, we invited him back several times. With each appearance, both on and off the air, we learned more and more about the realities of domestic abuse and violence.

Because Don is a Christian who knows the Word of God, he had no problem giving straightforward, biblical counsel to women who found themselves being abused and violated by the men in their lives. He didn't buy the common myth that an abused woman can pray more, be more submissive, and eventually her husband will see the error of his ways. That's what I like about Don. He knows God, he knows people, and he knows this is a very difficult issue that will not bear up under pat answers.

As an author, a speaker at women's conferences, and a counselor, I was thrilled to hear a Christian man stand up and say to women, "You do not have to take that kind of treatment, and here is what you do!" There has been such a lack of this kind of good, clear-cut advice coming from men in authority. When I heard Don Stewart, everything within me said, "This man knows of what he speaks."

I am delighted that *Refuge: A Pathway Out of Domestic Violence and Abuse* is available as a handbook for those who encounter the nasty inevitabilities of this scourge of our homes. If you are a pastor or church lay leader, this book will be one of the most valuable tools in your library. It gives you facts and how tos, many of which you may not have time or even inclination to develop on your own. When you are confronted with domestic abuse among your parishioners, you now have some answers. You don't have to wonder; you are holding what you need right here in your hand.

If you are a therapist or counselor working with a client living in the confusion and pain of domestic abuse, you now have the tools to give to her. Don Stewart has put it all in a palatable form that anyone can take in and absorb. Readers of this book will be forever grateful for the wisdom, candor, and boldness expressed in these pages by this godly, experienced police officer.

My prayer is that you would never experience the agony of domestic violence. But if you do, you can find help in these pages, maybe even to save your life or the lives of those you love.

— Jan Silvious
Author of *Foolproofing Your Life:*
Wisdom for Untangling Your Most Difficult Relationships

Acknowledgments

To my Lord & Savior Jesus Christ—thank You for allowing me the privilege of sharing the truth of Your unconditional love and acceptance of hurting, wounded, and suffering people. May they come to know You as I have as a loving, forgiving, and tenderhearted God. Thank You for guiding me as I wrote this book. May You alone be glorified in all that I have written.

I want to express my deepest and sincerest gratitude to the following people:

To Pastor Jim and Maxine Erickson for your support and encouragement over the years in good times and bad. Your counseling and mentoring profoundly impacted my life. Thank you for modeling how a godly husband and wife should treat one another.

To Carolyn Capp for providing me with a mature senior citizen's godly perspective on the issues of abuse and for all the initial editing you did. You were a constant source of encouragement to me and I shall always be grateful to you.

To Laurie at the Wisconsin Coalition Against Family Violence for your inspiring commitment on behalf of victims and your own testimony of God's faithfulness to you in times of great peril.

To the four women who shared the painful memories of abuse that are found in this book and who helped me understand the great need for the church in America to become more involved in the healing process.

To the wonderful staff at New Hope Publishers who enthusiastically embraced this project and made it become a reality. You're the best!

To my three children, Dan, Jennifer, and Nick. You are the love of my life and I am a fortunate man to have you as my children.

To my wonderful wife Cheryl for the hundreds of hours you spent alone while I labored over this book. Your patience and support made a difficult task much easier. Thank you for your patience with me these past 34 years as God continues to work in my life, developing me into a better husband, father, and man.

Introduction

Refuge: A Pathway Out of Domestic Violence and Abuse was written primarily for three reasons. First and foremost, I felt God calling me to take 25 years of training, experience, and skills developed as a Christian police officer and do something to try and reduce the devastation and destruction caused by family violence in our society.

The second reason was to tell people that God has not turned a deaf ear to their cries for help. He is faithful, He has heard you, and He has a plan for your life...a plan for good and not for evil. God never intended for our relationships to be violent, but sin entered in and has taken a terrible toll on us all. It is my deepest hope that this book will point the hurting, the abused, and the lost to a Savior named Jesus Christ, who is able to meet their every need and satisfy the longings of their soul. May the hurting and abused discover that God is able to provide a way of escape through the violence, and that He can heal the wounds that have been inflicted on them. Help is on the way.

The third reason for writing this book was to provide encouragement and guidance for the pastors and churches that labor so diligently to meet the needs of their people. Each day across this country, untold thousands of acts of benevolence are done quietly by pastors who try their best to help the battered and abused. This book will provide a common-sense approach to help churches minister to the needs of families in conflict and crisis.

Pastors I have spoken to tell me that in counseling, men and women will confide almost anything to them except family violence. Because it feels shameful, it is often kept secret out of embarrassment, shame, and fear. Some churches, on the other hand, have told women that they must remain married to the abuser because the Bible says so.

That misunderstanding of Scripture must be debunked now before one more woman ends up dead.

If I can convince just one church in every state in America of the tremendous need for expanded ministry in the area of domestic abuse, and if I can help that church to train its lay people to meet that need, this book will have made a difference.

The need is enormous and the challenge is great, but this kind of ministry provides the church with an incredible opportunity to introduce a loving Savior to a large and hurting segment of the population. This is also a challenge to believers in each church to step up to the plate and play an active role in giving generously to women and children who are in great need.

I am fortunate indeed to have been married to my wife Cheryl for the last 34 years and to be a father of three grown children—Dan, Jennifer, and Nick. I am truly blessed to have a peaceful home with a faithful wife and partner. But a growing number of women and children live in dread and fear every day of their lives, never knowing when the man of the house is going to come home and fly into another rage. I have arrived at a point in my career where I have seen one too many battered women, and one too many terrified and brokenhearted children crying as Daddy is hauled off to jail or prison and Mommy is on the way to the hospital. I have looked into their eyes filled with terror, and I hate what I see and feel. There are too many brokenhearted children who cry themselves to sleep every night, listening to Mommy being beaten up or sexually assaulted by her own husband.

So many women and children are trapped with little or no hope. So many children bring the baggage of fear, anxiety, depression, eating disorders, mistrust, low self-esteem, anger, and more into their adult lives and marriage relationships as a result of family violence. Too many kids grow up believing God looks like their violent dad. The lie must be exposed and the cycle must be broken.

The strength of our nation depends on the strength of our families, so the violence must be reduced if we are to thrive as a people. This book will provide you with a plan of action and show you a pathway out of the violence. The very heart of God must be deeply grieved to see the damage men and women are inflicting upon one another and their children within the framework of His sacred design for marriage.

Refuge: A Pathway Out of Domestic Violence and Abuse is a book of hope and encouragement for women caught in the web of violence. It is not intended as a substitute for qualified counseling and does not encourage divorce without exhausting all other remedies. Whenever possible, contact your local police department, crisis center, or family violence shelter for additional guidance before making any sudden or drastic changes in a relationship with a domestic violence abuser.

If you are living with a physically abusive partner, this book will assist you in getting out of that violent environment so you can deal with the situation from a position of strength and safety while surrounded by people who can guide you in wise decision-making.

It is my hope that God will be glorified in this book, that the abused will run to His loving arms and find refuge, healing, and renewal, that the church will be enlightened, and that the world will come to know that we care enough to confront this terrible problem.

May God richly bless you.

In peace,
Donald Stewart

CHAPTER 1

Family Violence and Betrayal from the Beginning

Today in the United States, crimes of violence committed against women are staggering. As a former Detective Sergeant in the investigation division of a police department, I worked on the front lines of family violence. I worked the night shift for 16 of my 25 years as a police officer, and investigated many domestic violence-related crimes. I have dealt with countless victims and suspects, and have seen everything—murder, sexual assault, beatings, false imprisonment, criminal damage to property, theft, stalking, and harassment.

Eventually, domestic violence became my focus as a police officer. I earned national certification from the Federal Law Enforcement Training Center as a domestic violence trainer for police officers, helping them to respond effectively to domestic violence calls.

I am also a Christian man. I've been trained as an Ambassador for Promise Keepers, I've led men's ministries in my church, and led accountability groups and Bible studies for men. As a Christian man, the violence against women I have seen makes me deeply angry. I have personally witnessed the suffering and pain domestic violence brings to families. This is not God's will, and so many forces in our world conspire to allow it to continue. As a Christian man, I want to do all I can to help these battered women and to stop the abuse.

The abuse of women and domestic violence in general is a worldwide disgrace, and America is just as guilty as any other country. If left unchecked for much longer, it will destroy the very fabric of our nation and eventually compromise our national security—a nation is only as strong as its families. Let's look at some alarming facts associated with abuse here in the United States.

An act of domestic violence occurs every 12 seconds. A National Crime Victimization study by the U.S. Department of Justice done from 1992–1996 reported the following facts:

- Approximately 2,000 American women are murdered each year by intimates (current or former spouses or romantic partners).
- On average, between 1992–1996, there were 960,000 violent victimizations of women age 12 and older by an intimate.
- Between 1976 and 1996, 31,260 women were intimate murder victims; 64% were killed by their husbands, 5% by ex-husbands, and 32% by non-marital partners such as boyfriends.
- About three out of every four women experiencing violence at the hands of an intimate report that the offense occurred at or near their own home. Half reported that it occurred between 6:00 P.M. and midnight.
- One third experienced an act of domestic violence more than once in the previous six months.

Also consider the following facts:

- The American College of Obstetricians and Gynecologists said three to four million women are beaten in their homes every year, but this number only refers to women hurt so severely that they received medical attention and called the police.

- The abusive man generally maintains a public image as a friendly, caring person who is a devoted "family man."
- Children who witness their mother's abuse often take on delinquent and violent behavior.
- 85% of batterers watched domestic violence occur in their own homes as children and/or experienced child sexual or physical abuse.
- Violence in the home is considered the root cause of violence in the streets
- Batterers are often seductive and charming when they are not being violent.
- 80% of runaway children are from violent homes.
- Nearly half of all men who abuse their female partners also abuse their children.
- Women who are being battered are less able to care for their children.
- Battering is the single largest cause of injury to women.
- Of boys aged 11–20 years old who commit homicide, 63% kill a man who was abusing their mothers.
- Men commit 95% of all domestic violence assaults.
- 50% of all willful homicides of females are committed by a past or present intimate partner.
- 15–25% of all battered females are pregnant. The March of Dimes reports that more babies are now born with birth defects as a result of the mother being battered during pregnancy than from the combination of all the diseases and illnesses for which we immunize pregnant women.
- Battered women are two times more likely than men to commit suicide.
- Battery is the single largest cause of injury to women—more frequent than auto accidents, muggings, and rapes combined.
- Women in the US are in nine times more danger in their own homes than they are in the street.
- Children who have witnessed abuse themselves are 1000 times more likely to abuse a spouse/partner or a child when they become adults

than children raised in non-abusive homes.

- According to the U.S. Department of Justice, an estimated 1,007,000 women are stalked annually.
- Four women in five who were stalked by a current husband or live-in boyfriend were also attacked; nearly 40% of those attacks included forced sex.

If those facts don't alarm you, then I don't know what will. Domestic violence and battery of women in general is costing us all dearly and sapping our national vitality. Every woman who is being beaten and abused is someone's daughter, sister, mother, or wife. The financial cost of emergency room care, hospitalization, psychiatric treatment, counseling, lost wages from missed work, and rehabilitation is estimated by the National Crime Victim survey to cost victims $150,000,000 per year.

Additionally, consider the cost of maintaining family violence shelters, crisis centers, Family Court hearings, Child Protection Agencies, police, courts, prosecutors, and prisons. On and on the list goes of public services that must exist to respond to the problem.

Consider the emotional devastation that is being done to the victim, her children, the victim's parents, and other family members. Oftentimes the victim loses her job when she can't get to work because she's been injured once again by her husband, or shows up at work with a black eye or teeth knocked out.

She finds the tires on her car slashed, sugar dumped in the fuel tank, or the windshield smashed out, and she has no insurance or money to get the car fixed. Or her assailant shows up at her place of employment and creates a scene in front of everyone to humiliate her in the workplace. It's usually only a matter of time before the employer begins to fear for his/her own safety and the safety of the other employees. He realizes that if he gets rid of the abused woman, the problem will stop showing up at work and he can return to business as usual.

Without a network of caring people to assist the victim and her children through the difficulty, she is most likely destined to a life of hopelessness and fear. Without a decent job or a car to get to work, many victims end up homeless, unemployed, and mentally overloaded. Some turn to prostitution, alcoholism, drug addiction, shoplifting, check fraud, forgery, or burglary. Others struggle with depression, thoughts of suicide, anxiety attacks, eating disorders, and more abusive relationships. The effects of domestic abuse on children are also enormous and will be addressed later in the book.

I have often wondered what happens in a woman's life between the time she was a happy little girl, skipping down the sidewalk, and now as a battered woman. Was she also a victim of physical or sexual abuse as a child? Was she told she was stupid or ugly or unwanted? Did she grow up in a home witnessing her father abuse her mother and come to believe that women are supposed to give up total control of their lives to the person they marry?

At what point did she surrender her dignity and self respect to her abuser, and why did she do it? Was she taught in church that she was to submit to her husband no matter what? Has she stayed with her abuser because of a belief that the kids would be better off with both parents than with only one?

Violence Against Women in the Bible

The Bible tells countless stories about violence against women—oftentimes sanctioned by the culture of the time. Amnon, one of King David's sons, was half-brother to David's beautiful daughter Tamar. In 2 Samuel 13:11–18, we learn how Amnon pretended to be bedridden with an illness in order to lure Tamar into his bedroom.

> "When she brought them to him to eat, he took hold of her and said to her, 'Come, lie with me, my sister.' But she answered him, 'No, my brother, do not violate me, for such a thing is not done in Israel; do not do this disgraceful thing! As for me, where could I get rid of my reproach? And as for you, you will be like one of the fools in Israel. Now therefore, please speak to the king, for he will not

withhold me from you.' However, he would not listen to her; since he was stronger than she, he violated her and lay with her. Then Amnon hated her with a very great hatred; for the hatred with which he hated her was greater than the love with which he had loved her. And Amnon said to her, 'Get up, go away!' But she said to him, 'No, because this wrong in sending me away is greater than the other that you have done to me!' Yet he would not listen to her. Then he called his young man who attended him and said, 'Now throw this woman out of my presence, and lock the door behind her.'"

Amnon betrayed Tamar through his lust.

In the Book of Judges, chapter 19, we read a story of a man who traveled from the hill country of Ephraim to Bethlehem looking for his concubine, who had run away four months earlier. After staying five days at the home of the concubine's father, the man, his servant, and his concubine traveled to Gibeah, where they stayed for the night in the house of an old man who lived nearby. In verses 22–29, we read:

"While they were celebrating, behold, the men of the city, certain worthless fellows, surrounded the house, pounding the door; and they spoke to the owner of the house, the old man, saying, 'Bring out the man who came into your house that we may have relations with him.' Then the man, the owner of the house, went out to them and said to them, 'No, my fellows, please do not act so wickedly; since this man has come into my house, do not commit this act of folly. Here is my virgin daughter and his concubine. Please let me bring them out that you may ravish them and do to them whatever you wish. But do not commit such an act of folly against this man.' But the men would not listen to him. So the man seized his concubine and brought her out to them; and they raped her and abused her all night until morning, then let her go at the approach of dawn."

The next morning, the concubine was found dead at the door, her hands stretched toward the threshold. **This woman was abandoned to the sexual desires of a mob.**

In the 8th chapter of John we find the story of the woman who is caught in the act of adultery and is about to be stoned by a crowd of male Pharisees and scribes. Her life is saved because Jesus intervenes. Notice that the man who committed the act of adultery was not dragged out to be stoned to death, only the woman. **The woman was betrayed by religious hypocrites.**

Throughout history, across nations and cultures, and even to this very day, women are still being used and abused in ways that God never intended. For centuries the Chinese bound the feet of women so they could barely walk. Even today female babies in China are routinely killed, starved to death, or dumped in orphanages and left to die because their parents wanted a male child. In India, women are burned to death, mutilated by having acid thrown in their faces, or sold into prostitution by men who think they have no value as wives or children. In many Muslim cultures women are forced to walk around in public with their faces covered with a veil. Violation of this custom could result in a public flogging or death. Even today in many middle eastern societies the killing of a woman often goes unpunished if she was killed for something that is perceived as bringing disgrace on the family. In some parts of Africa, young girls are held down by tribal elders and circumcised—mutilated to prevent them from ever enjoying sex. In Thailand, girls as young as ten years of age are sold by their fathers to flesh peddlers to be enjoyed by foreign men who travel oversees by the planeload for erotic vacations of sex with a child virgin. In times of war, women have always been taken captive and used and abused by invading armies of men.

Since the beginning of time, men have sought to forcefully impose their will on women in order to serve their own needs and desires. Women have been raped, murdered, burned, sexually assaulted, mutilated, drowned, tortured, and exploited. Men have beaten, strangled, starved, kicked, punched, choked, and restrained their freedom of movement. Women have been forced into bondage, slavery, pornography, drug addiction, and unwanted pregnancy, and they are often the unwitting recipients of sexually transmitted diseases from unfaithful husbands. They have been betrayed and abandoned by scurrilous men who used them up, emptied them out, and dumped them like the weekly trash at the curb. Often they are left to support themselves and their children with nothing more than the clothes on their backs.

The Christian church around the world has a shameful history of contributing to the abuse of women and ignoring their cries for help. It is quite possible that, over the centuries, more innocent women have been murdered in the name of God or religion than for all other reasons combined.

A Short History of Abuse

In the 1500s, men were exhorted from the pulpit to beat their wives; morality tales were told of the wickedness of a nagging wife and the proper punishment for such behavior. In the mid-fifteenth century, Friar Cherubino of Siena compiled the "Rules of Marriage," which said: "When you see your wife commit an offense, don't rush at her with insults and violent blows...Scold her sharply, bully and terrify her. And if this still doesn't work...take up a stick and beat her soundly, for it is better to punish the body and correct the soul than damage the soul and spare the body...Then readily beat her, not in rage but out of charity and concern for her soul, so that the beating will redound to your merit and her good."

In the 17th century, British jurist Lord Hale wrote that a husband could not be found guilty of raping his wife. A wife, he explained, had given herself in marriage to her husband. The common law reasons: 1) the wife is chattel belonging to her husband, 2) husband and wife are "one" and obviously a husband cannot rape himself, and 3) by marriage the wife consents to intercourse with her husband on a continuing basis. Not until the 1980s did the "marital rape exception rule" begin to erode.

British jurist Sir William Blackstone, in his *Commentaries on the Laws of England*, influenced the development of early American law. He commented on the "rule of thumb," which permitted a man to beat his wife with a "rod not thicker than his thumb." Blackstone defined women's "very being or legal existence...suspended during marriage or at least incorporated or consolidated into that of the husband, under whose wing, protection and cover, she performs everything." Early colonial settlers routinely beat their spouses using the rule of thumb standard, except on Sundays, when beating your wife was prohibited.

In 1824 in North Carolina, a court upheld a husband's right to use force when he choked his wife, stating that: "The law permits him to use towards his wife such a degree of force, as is necessary to control unruly temper, and make her behave herself; and unless some permanent injury be inflicted, or there be an excess of violence, or such degree of cruelty as shows that it is inflicted to gratify his own bad passions, the law will not invade the domestic forum, or go behind the curtain. It prefers to leave the parties to themselves."

In 1874, in North Carolina: "If no permanent injury has been inflicted, nor malice, cruelty nor dangerous violence shown by the husband, it is better to draw the curtain, shut out the public gaze and leave the parties to forget and forgive or kill each other."

In his book *Violence Against Wives*, Emerson Dobash writes:

"Religious leaders placed faith in the idea that the subjection of wives, which they supported strongly, could be achieved by teaching women it was their sacred duty to obey and by vesting husbands with great authority to control them. Flogging was used throughout society as a means of controlling the powerless: children, women, and the middle classes. Female oppression was determined by the birch....Although the theologians used the moral order, social pressure, and fear of eternal damnation to win compliance from wives and discouraged wife beating, it was widespread. Throughout the seventeenth, eighteenth, and nineteenth centuries there was little objection within the community to a man using force against his wife as long as he did not exceed certain tacit limits....A woman could be beaten if she behaved 'shamelessly' and caused jealousy, was lazy, unwilling to work in the fields, became drunk, spent too much money, or neglected the house. The community agreed that these were offenses that merited, even required, punishment as long as the physical force was restricted to 'blows, thumps, kicks or punches on the back if they leave no lasting traces.' Men were not allowed to use 'sharp edged or crushing instruments,' that is, weapons, especially cleavers, axes, sickles, or knives. Nor was it considered appropriate to direct blows at the head or sensitive vital organs (breast or stomach), and maltreatment by a husband during pregnancy or after birth was always cited with great indignation. It was the moderate use of physical punishment that separated the 'reasonable husband from the brute.'"

Sometimes these battered women have attempted to defend themselves. In her book *Justifiable Homicide: Battered Women, Self-Defense, and The Law*, Cynthia Gillespie writes:

"In medieval times few women were killed outside their homes. Indeed, the great majority were killed inside their homes. Considering that wife beating was common and the home was such a lethal place for women, many of these homicides [wives killing husbands] must certainly have been in self-defense; but two aspects of medieval family law kept them from being considered as such. The first was that a woman lived her entire life 'under the rod' of men. Her husband, just like her father, had the right to beat her all he wished, as long as he was doing it for her own good, as punishment for wrongdoing, or to keep her from falling into error. Even though he was not supposed to beat her seriously enough to maim or kill her, his right of chastisement was so taken for granted that little was probably done about it if he did. One commentator tells the story of an early fifteenth-century Hampshire man who beat and kicked his wife to death. He was put on trial, but the jury acquitted him and had it entered into the official records that the poor woman had died of the plague.

"The second aspect of medieval family law was that a woman's relation to her husband was that of a subject to his lord. He was her 'baron' and she owed him absolute fealty and obedience. If he killed her in cold blood, it might be murder; but if she killed him, she was guilty of treason. The punishment for that was the same as if she had killed the king. She was burned alive at the stake, a horror that persisted at least until 1763 when a woman named Ann Bedington was executed in this manner at Ipswitch."

Domestic Violence Today

Perhaps because it has been such a deeply ingrained practice, domestic violence is often hidden behind a veil of secrecy and shame. People are often shocked to find that their neighbor, their sister, someone in the church pew next to them has been suffering regular beatings for years. We almost sense that domestic violence is something that doesn't happen to people we know. Don't you believe it. Let's take a look at the profiles of the abuser and the abused.

CHAPTER 2

Profile of
the Abuser

Abusers come in every size, shape, age, race, income level, occupation, and sex. Many of them have been abused as children, but some have not. Some domestic violence offenders have a prior criminal history for a variety of offenses, but many others have no criminal record at all, except for domestic violence. My job as a criminal investigator required that I spend a great deal of time interviewing men who had committed crimes that range from murder to sexual assault to domestic violence. Part of that time was spent in our jail and in the Wisconsin prison system. After interviewing at least several hundred men and also ministering to prisoners as a guest of the chaplain, I have come to believe that most men who commit crimes are suffering from the effects of what I call the "father wound." The bottom line is unresolved conflict or anger between father and son, or father and daughter.

I am not a psychologist and won't pretend to be one in this book, but I am a trained observer. Part of my job is to listen to the tiniest details that may seem insignificant to others, but often hold the keys to understanding the motivation behind the crime. Our prisons are filled with men and women who are suffering from the father wound. Let me give you just two examples of what the father wound looks like.

Paul's Story

"I was just 11 years old when my church youth group planned a father-son campout. I could hardly wait to go with my dad because he was rarely ever home. It seemed like all he did was work, and when he was home he never did much with me because he was usually talking on the phone with one of his golfing buddies or taking care of business. Dad didn't go to church with Mom and me, but the church said it was okay for my dad to come with the group if he wanted to. I could hardly wait to get home and ask my dad if he would go. I was really looking forward to pitching a tent with him, sitting around the campfire, cooking food, and having fun. I waited for him to come home and gave him all the information—he agreed to go. I was so excited because I had always wanted to go fishing and camping and do things with my dad like other kids did with theirs.

"The day of the campout finally arrived, and I had all our gear in the garage, ready to load in his car the minute he came home. We were supposed to meet at the church at 5:00 P.M. and carpool to the camping area. But Dad didn't get home from work until 7:00 P.M. I was in a panic.

"He explained that he got hung up at work and told me not to worry, that 'We could get up early tomorrow morning and join the others then.' I was really disappointed but tried to make the best of it. I hardly slept all night. I was up at 5:00 A.M. and had everything in his trunk while it was still getting light out, all ready to catch up with the other kids and their dads. Dad had said we could leave by 7:00 A.M. and I was ready almost two hours before that. But he never even came out of his bedroom until 9:00 A.M.

"When he saw me standing out front with the camping gear, he explained to me that he had a bad back and couldn't sleep on the ground. He hoped that I would understand and that I'd be a 'big boy' about it...but could I please get my things out of his car, because he had to take care of some important matters at the office.

"Unloading that car was one of the most painful things I've ever done in my life. I had wanted to go camping with him so badly. And then, while I was putting my stuff away in the storage area and he thought I couldn't see, I watched him load his golf clubs into the trunk of his car and drive away to take care of his 'important matter' at the office. That's when I realized my dad never intended to go with me in the first place. He was a liar, and I found out how little I meant to him. His pattern of breaking promises to me continued throughout my teenage years. Now, as an adult, I have just completely shut him out of my life and want nothing to do with him.

"When I grew up I struggled with such low self-esteem and insecurity about who I was that I have always lacked confidence in myself. I never felt like my dad affirmed my worth. It was like I just existed but I never understood why. I find myself emotionally distant and constantly angry with my wife and kids. I have come so close to striking my wife that it frightens me. Pornography has secretly controlled a large part of my life, and I see God as distant and cold and wonder where He is in all of this, if He exists at all. I struggle to show my kids that I love them, and can't seem to show any tender emotions when I'm in front of them."

The father wound in this country is so huge that it crosses all cultures, economic barriers, age groups, and races. The following story will give you some idea of just how deep and widespread the effects of the wound are.

Several years ago a nun working in a state prison for men asked several inmates if they would like her to get them a greeting card so they could send a card home to their moms on Mother's Day. The men eagerly accepted the nun's offer, and soon the word spread that the dear sister was getting cards to send out. The nun had so many requests that she contacted one of the major greeting card companies and asked them if they would donate 500+ Mother's Day cards. The greeting card company granted her request and donated just over 500 cards to the inmates. Soon every prisoner except a handful had sent out cards to their mothers.

The nun was so overwhelmed by the response that she thought it would be a great idea to see if the men wanted Father's Day cards to send out also. This time the response was painfully different. Out of a prison of just over 500 men, only a handful was willing to send a card to their dads. I've spent a good deal of time talking to men in institutions, so this did not surprise me when I heard it. I have had convicts tell me that they have never seen or heard from their father since the day they were locked up. One prisoner told me that the only letter he had ever received from his dad was a letter telling him to change his name so that when he gets out of prison no one will know that he is his father's son.

Many of the men I've spoken to have told me that if they had just had a father to affirm their worth, love them, discipline them appropriately, and hold them accountable for their behavior as kids, they might not have ended up in prison. A high percentage of the men in prison don't know or care who their fathers are, but every one of them is deeply wounded by the absence of a father's love and affection.

Street-hardened kids I have worked with tell me that the reason they joined a gang is because the gang cared about them and accepted them unconditionally. Someone spent time with them and demanded accountability and obedience to a standard of conduct. The gang was the family they lacked, and the gang leader became the authority figure they wanted. The member, after breaking a rule, would subject himself or herself to oftentimes-harsh discipline and other sanctions imposed upon them by the leaders because the gang was where they got their sense of identity.

The thing every one of them had in common was the lack of a father in his life and an intense hatred for his father if he knew who he was. Most of them had the attitude that, "Dad, you could beat me, neglect me, or abuse me when I was a little kid, but now I'm big enough to hurt you or hurt someone else. I'll show you what I'm capable of. I'll get your attention one way or the other."

Many of the young men I talked to were motivated to commit crimes just to get even with their fathers. They all had very high anger levels combined with noticeable sadness because of their dads, and many of them felt isolated and alone.

Another thing these gang members had in common was absolutely no sense of right or wrong. If they knew the difference, they didn't care because they had no moral foundation under them. If it felt good, they'd do it. If they wanted someone else's property, they would just take it. All of them lacked a good role model for how a husband, father, and man should behave. For many of them, the only thing they ever saw their father do was beat them, assault their mother, come home drunk, break their promises—and their father never told them how much he loved or appreciated them. Most of their fathers were emotionally absent, unpredictable, dictatorial, and unreasonable. Many that I talked to had never been to church and knew nothing of God. I heard a number of them say, "I swore I'd never turn out like my old man, but I guess I did."

Our juvenile detention facilities are packed with brokenhearted boys and girls because of the father wound. They will enter adulthood angry, wounded, and determined to get even without even realizing why. They will be the next generation of wife beaters, child abusers, murderers, rapists, and armed robbers, who feel worthless and unwanted. They will spend their lives unconsciously looking for the approval and acceptance of their father, who never affirmed their worth.

For those who do not fall into a life of crime, many will become workaholics, trying to become successful in order to gain their father's approval. In their thirst for a father's blessing, they will sacrifice their wives and kids to the god of money, power, and influence. Some will become prominent in the church and community and will quietly batter their wives, who will be forced to live under their dictatorial and controlling hand.

Many will take reckless chances in business, risking family finances and the stability of their homes in order to climb the ladder to the top. In their wake will be a trail littered with wounded children who may never have been physically abused, but are nonetheless empty and hurting from the emotional absence and lack of moral leadership from their father.

The Verbal Abuser

There is a great deal that can be said about the verbal abuser. This is the category of abuse that most men inflict upon their partners. In some ways its effects are far more damaging than the wounds that come from physical violence. Here is a man who smugly says, "I would never hit a woman," but thinks nothing of demoralizing or humiliating her with his words. The abuser is usually a master put-down artist, capable of inflicting painful wounds upon his victim. He generally knows where she's most vulnerable and attacks her there. If she's struggling with something in her physical appearance, he may call her fat or ugly. If she didn't finish high school, he may call her stupid, ignorant, a dropout, etc. If she's been laid off from a job or didn't get a promotion, she may hear herself being described as a loser. Most important to remember is that most verbal abuse has no basis in fact—thin women are often told they are fat, and smart women are often told they are stupid.

The verbal abuser usually has a label or a tag for everything that doesn't please him, and the tag is almost always a negative one that puts down the other person in an effort to build himself up. The verbal abuser is highly controlling and will scream, shout, threaten, and intimidate his partner very effectively. That same person who behaves this way when he is in the house alone with you or the children usually doesn't behave this way if he is in a subordinate role at work. The reason he tempers his remarks in the workplace is that he knows he will be challenged and dealt with by someone more powerful than he is.

If the verbal abuser is the owner of a company or is in a position of great authority at work, it will be common for him to behave the same way in the workplace. As a result of his verbally abusive behavior, he often finds himself hiring a never-ending stream of new victims to scream at and humiliate. Verbal abusers leave a trail of hurt as wide as a highway, with victims who can still vividly recall the biting sarcasm and criticism even decades later.

I know a woman who is married to a police officer who is a foul-mouthed man who has never had a good word to say about his wife or anyone else since the day they were married. In public he verbally demolishes her to such an extent that people don't want to even greet them. The way he talks to her, and about her, makes them feel so uncomfortable that they will avoid this couple because they feel so badly for his wife.

What is sad about this relationship is that the wife has absolutely no sense of self-worth or confidence, and neither do the man's daughters. He has a critical and sarcastic spirit that is unequaled by anything I have ever seen. Despite this, if you ask his wife how she can tolerate such awful treatment she will tell you, "He's just a lovable blowhard—he doesn't mean anything by it." This woman has created an excuse for her husband's destructive behavior.

As long as she can create a false identity for her husband, she doesn't have to face the truth that he is a cruel, mean-spirited, self-centered person who will continue to take advantage of her passivity. This woman is in denial and will never know the joy and value of her own self-worth. In his workplace, this raging bull is a cowardly cop who tears down management behind their backs, but is afraid to speak his mind to their faces.

The Sexual Abuser

In *The Male Batterer* by Daniel Jay Sonkin, Del Martin, and Lenore E. A. Walker, the authors state that rape frequently occurs in a battering relationship. Research indicates that 59% of battered women in a sample of more than 400 had been forced to have sex, and for 49% it happened more than once. A total of 41% had been forced to perform unusual sex acts. They were tied up, threatened with a gun, beaten, or intimidated to act out the sexual fantasies of their batterers. The acts included insertion of objects into their vaginas, group sex, sex with animals, bondage, and sadomasochistic activities.

Most research on rape shows that it is not primarily an expression of sexual desire; it is the use of sexuality to express power and anger. The "power rape," according to Nicholas Groth, is the most common form. In his book *Men Who Rape*, he describes the "power assertive" rapist as using rape to express virility, mastery, and dominance. The "power reassurance" rapist, on the other hand, rapes to resolve doubts about his sexual adequacy and masculinity. The "anger" rape is particularly brutal, and in extreme cases may result in murder. The "anger retaliation" rapist expresses his hostility toward women. His motivation is revenge, degradation, and humiliation. The "anger excitation" rapist finds pleasure, thrills, and excitement in his victim's suffering. He hurts and tortures his victim to punish her.

Groth might as well have been describing batterers. They certainly fit the categories: assertion of power to express dominance or remove doubts about his masculinity, the expression of anger as a retaliation against women, and the excitement engendered by seeing his victim suffer.

The Physical Abuser:
Signs to Look For in a Battering Personality

Many women want to be able to predict whether the man they are about to become involved with might become physically abusive. Below is a list of behaviors that are seen in people who beat their girlfriends or wives. The last four signs are almost always seen only if the person is a batterer. If the person has several of the other behaviors (say three or more), there is a strong potential for physical violence. The more signs the person has, the more likely the person is a batterer. In some cases a batterer may have only a couple of behaviors that you will recognize, but they are very exaggerated, such as extreme jealousy over ridiculous things. Initially the batterer will try to explain his behavior as signs of his love and concern, and you may be flattered, but as time goes on the behavior will become more severe and serve to dominate you. Here are the signs that should alert you to a potentially abusive person.

Jealousy. At the beginning of a relationship, an abuser will always say that jealousy is a sign of love. Jealousy has nothing to do with love—it's a sign of insecurity and possessiveness. He will question you about people you talk to, accuse you of flirting, or become jealous of the time you spend with your family, friends, or children. As his jealousy progresses, he may call you frequently during the day or drop by unexpectedly. He may refuse to let you work for fear that you'll meet someone else. He may check your car mileage to see how far you've traveled, and ask his friends to watch you.

Controlling behavior. At first, the batterer will say that he behaves as he does because he's concerned for your safety, your need to use your time well, or your need to make good decisions. He will be angry if you are late coming back from the store or an appointment. He may question you about where you went and who you talked to. As this behavior gets worse, he may not let you make personal decisions about the house, your clothes, or the church you attend. He may keep all of the money or make you ask permission to leave the house or the room.

Quick involvement. Many battered women dated or knew their abuser for less than six months before they were engaged or lived together. He comes on like a whirlwind, claiming "love at first sight." He will tell you flattering things such as, "You're the only person I could ever talk to," or "I've never felt loved like this by anyone before." He needs someone desperately, and he will pressure you to commit to him.

Unrealistic expectations. He is very dependent on you for all his needs. He expects you to be the perfect wife, mother, friend, and lover. He will say things like, "If you love me, I'm all you need—you're all I need." You are expected to take care of everything for him emotionally and in the home.

Isolation. He will try and cut you off from all resources. If you have men friends, he may label you a "whore"; if you have women friends, he may label you a "lesbian"; if you are close to your family, you will be accused of having "apron strings." He will accuse people who support you of causing trouble and may want you to live in the country without a phone. He may not let you use the car or allow you to go to school.

Blames others for his problems. He may be chronically unemployed, and someone is always doing him wrong or is out to get him. When he makes mistakes, he blames you for upsetting him and keeping him from concentrating on his job. He will tell you that you are at fault for almost anything that goes wrong.

Blames others for the way he feels. He will tell you, "You make me mad," or "You're hurting me by not doing what I want you to do," or "I can't help getting angry at you." He really makes the decision about what he thinks and feels but will use his feelings to manipulate you. He accuses people of "pressing his buttons."

Hypersensitivity. He is easily insulted and claims his feelings are hurt when he's actually mad, or he takes the slightest setbacks as personal attacks. He will rant and rave about the injustice of things that have happened to him—everyday things such as being asked to work overtime or getting a parking ticket. Every wrong that occurs to him is personified and is an excuse to "set him off."

Cruelty to animals or children. Here is a man who punishes animals cruelly or is insensitive to their pain or suffering. He may expect children to be capable of doing things far beyond their ability (for example, he whips a two-year-old for wetting a diaper) or may tease children or younger brothers and sisters until they cry. He may not want the children to eat at the table, or he may demand that the children be kept in their room all evening while he is at home. Sixty percent of men who beat the women they are with also beat their children.

"Playful" use of force in sex. This man will throw you down and hold you down during sex, and he will want to act out fantasies during sex where you are helpless. He is unconsciously letting you know that the idea of rape is exciting to him. He has little regard about whether or not you want to have sex, and he uses anger to gain your compliance. He will demand sex when you're asleep, ill, or tired.

Verbal abuse. In addition to saying things that are meant to be cruel and hurtful, this can be seen when the abuser degrades you by cursing at you or running down your accomplishments. The abuser will tell you that you are stupid and unable to function without him. This may involve the abuser waking you up during a sound sleep to verbally abuse you, or he may not allow you to go to sleep.

Rigid gender roles. The abuser expects you to serve him. He may tell you that you are to stay at home, that you must obey him in all things, even if he orders you to do things that are cruel. The abuser will see you as inferior to him, responsible for menial tasks, stupid, and unable to be a whole person without a relationship.

Dr. Jekyll and Mr. Hyde. Many women are confused by their abuser's sudden changes in mood. You may think the abuser has some special mental problem because one minute he's nice and the next minute he's exploding. Explosiveness and moodiness are typical of people who beat their partners, and these behaviors are related to other behaviors such as hypersensitivity. This switching keeps you on guard or "walking on eggshells."

Past battering. This person may say that he has hit a woman in the past but that she made him do it. You may hear from friends, family, or coworkers that he is abusive. A batterer will beat you if you are with him long enough for the violence to begin; situational circumstances do not make a person have an abusive personality. He may acknowledge past violence, but will tell you the victim or the police "exaggerated" its severity or "blew it out of proportion."

Threats of violence. He may threaten physical force to control you—"I'll kill you," or "I'll break your neck." Most people do not threaten their mates. A batterer will try to excuse such threats by saying, "Everybody talks like that." This is not true.

Breaking or striking objects. This behavior is used as a punishment (breaking loved possessions) but is used mostly to terrorize you into submission. The abuser might slam his fists on the table or throw objects around or near you. This is very noteworthy behavior. Not only is it a sign of extreme emotional immaturity, but there's a great danger when someone thinks they have the "right" to punish or frighten you.

Any force during an argument. This may involve a batterer holding you down, physically restraining your freedom of movement, or any pushing or shoving. Holding you against a wall and saying, "You're going to listen to me," is not acceptable.

The Cycle of Violence

According to Lenore Walker's book *The Battered Woman*, an abusive relationship typically follows a cycle that is marked by three well-recognized phases. Although there are some variations from this cycle, many abusive relationships will repeat this cycle over and over.

The tension building phase is a period of time when a wife either avoids her husband or frantically works to keep her husband's world running smoothly. She does this to prevent triggering another abusive explosion. In this way, she holds some limited control in the relationship. Sometimes there are minor skirmishes, but the wife suppresses her anger by either blaming herself ("I should have kept quiet about the credit card bill"), by blaming something in the man's environment ("He must have had a tough day at work"), or reasoning that it could have been worse. Each time a small abusive incident occurs, tension in the relationship increases. A nagging sense of helplessness begins to overwhelm her. Eventually the tension simmers to a boil, bringing on the next phase. Ordinarily, this first phase lasts for long periods of time.

The acute battering or abusive phase is earmarked by increased severity of abuse. Unlike the minor abusive incidents that occurred in the first phase, the incidents in this phase are far more caustic. This phase is usually triggered by some particular event or set of circumstances, though they are rarely the same and often unpredictable. Like a violent storm that strikes on a clear, sunny day, the physical attack or verbal assault seems to come out of nowhere. A husband could be set off by a meal that was unsatisfactory or his wife's refusal to engage in sex. Normally this phase lasts from 2–24 hours.

Initially a woman is in a state of shock and disbelief. It's difficult for her to come to grips with what has happened to her. If she's been through the abusive cycle several times, she's likely to experience a mixture of relief and rage—relief that the inevitable assault is over, and rage over her husband's empty promises to stop. She may be faced with the need for medical treatment. She might report her husband to the authorities or inform family members of the abuse. Typically, however, she remains silent and doesn't expose her husband. Within her is an increasing sense of helplessness and feelings of self-hatred for not doing something to prevent the abuse.

The calm and penance phase, also called the coercion stage, is a time when the abuser appears to be stricken with grief over his cruel and insensitive actions. He works very hard to make up for what he's done with apparent acts of kindness, promising never to abuse again. Usually a wife welcomes this phase and enjoys the special attention given to her. Because she desperately wants to believe that her husband is sincere, she tends to overrate the genuineness of his remorse.

During this time she may drop criminal charges or shrink away from pursuing legal separation or divorce. She will frequently come up with "reasonable" explanations why her husband mistreated her. This phase may last a day or a few months, and it tends to become less and less common. Eventually the tensions will slowly begin to mount and the cycle will repeat.

Abruptly, the calm-and-penance phase is substituted with a **sudden-return-to-normal phase.** In this phase, there is often a significant period of silence. A wife may be hoping that her husband will apologize. But what usually happens is that her husband eventually begins to act as if nothing ever happened. The abusive incident is not mentioned and no apology is offered. Life just somehow goes back to normal. But because their problems are not exposed and worked through, the tension escalates, leading to another abusive episode.

Let's take a look at how an abuser's anger and his refusal to control it properly contribute to the three phases in the cycle of violence.

Anger Principles

Anger defined: Anger is an emotional response that tells us that we are dissatisfied with something in our life. It is designed to effect or cause a change in our situation. Anger expressed abusively or aggressively is designed to gain control over our situation or others. It is often considered a negative emotion for that reason.

Anger vs. aggression/abuse: There is much confusion about anger and aggression/abuse. While anger is an emotion that indicates dissatisfaction with someone, something, or circumstances in our lives, aggression/abuse is a behavioral response to anger. Anger and its expression are often confused because of the frequent association between anger and the way we learned that it is supposed to be expressed.

Loss of control myth: People do not lose control, they choose control. Anger expressed aggressively is designed to control others, to gain control of a situation. People use the degree of control necessary to get the desired response. If people really lost control, they would do much more serious injury and would not be able to stop.

Myth of provocation: People often believe they can be provoked to violence or aggressive behaviors. Once angered, you have a responsibility about how you express your anger. Justifiable anger does not justify abuse. You even make choices about what makes you angry.

Issue of power: People who perceive that they have very little power overuse what little power they have. The reality is that when you express your anger aggressively, you give away your power. You can be 100% right about the issue at hand, but you give away your right to hold the other person accountable because the focus has become you and your inability to deal with your anger appropriately.

Issue of choice: Seldom does an issue cause anger, but rather, it is your perception of the issue that makes you angry. Things do not make us mad—what we say to ourselves about those things does.

Anger-expressives vs. anger-retentives: People have different ways of dealing with anger. Some people express anger directly most of the time. These are the people who are frequently aggressive. They need to learn how to tone it down, to express their anger appropriately so that it does not hurt others. Some people stuff their anger inside when they get angry—these are the people who frequently withdraw when they get angry. They need to learn to express their anger safely so that it does not hurt themselves.

What is a temper? People often say they have a temper and that when they get mad they lose their temper. Actually, there is no such thing as a temper. We do not have this thing called a temper inside us that comes out at times of anger. Saying we have a temper is a convenient way of letting ourselves off the hook when we have expressed our anger aggressively or abusively. After all, if we have this temper and when we get angry we lose it, who could hold us accountable for that? Saying we have temper is a way to defend ourselves for behavior that is unacceptable, and it is a defense mechanism against having to change it.

Anger in the Bible

Let's take a look at just a few verses of Scripture and see what God has to say about anger.

> "Be angry, and yet not sin; do not let the sun go down on your anger, and do not give the devil an opportunity. He who steals must steal no longer; but rather he must labor, performing with his own hands what is good, so that he will have something to share with one who has need. Let no unwholesome word proceed from your mouth, but only such a word as is good for edification according to the need of the moment, so that it will give grace to those who hear. Do not grieve the Holy Spirit of God, by whom you were sealed for the day of redemption. Let all bitterness and wrath and anger and clamor and slander be put away from among you, along with all malice. Be kind to one another, tender hearted, forgiving each other, just as God in Christ also has forgiven you."
>
> —Ephesians 4:26–32

"An angry man stirs up strife, and a hot-tempered man abounds in transgression."

—Proverbs 29:22

"For the churning of milk produces butter, and pressing the nose brings forth blood; so the churning of anger produces strife."

—Proverbs 30:33

Domestic Violence Defined

Domestic violence is any abusive or coercive behavior used to control an intimate partner, including multiple kinds of actions. It is a pattern of manipulative and violent tactics that force the victim to change her behavior in response to the abuse. It occurs in current or former dating, married, or cohabiting relationships. Men are responsible for 95% of all acts of domestic violence in the United States.

Batterers seek to gain and maintain power and control over their intimate partners by the use of actual and assumed power. One of the best ways to understand tactics that an abuser often uses is to look at the "Power and Control" wheel developed by the Domestic Abuse Intervention Project in Duluth, Minnesota. (See Appendix A.) The core of the wheel is divided into the following eight categories, which represent the psychological tactics and emotionally abusive behaviors used by batterers: (1) emotional, (2) intimidation, (3) coercion and threats, (4) economic, (5) male privilege, (6) using children, (7) isolation, and (8) minimizing, denying, blaming. Although many acts of psychological and emotional abuse do not violate state or federal law, they serve as a means for the batterer to establish control. Control is often enforced physically and sexually.

A woman who witnesses her husband punch a hole in the wall with his fist in a moment of rage may remember that moment for the rest of her life. From that time on, to maintain control of his wife when he's mad, all the abuser might have to do is make a fist. The psychological trauma of seeing her husband put his fist through a wall, a door, or a window is often sufficient for him to maintain control over his wife without ever having to hit her.

Reasons Men Batter

The reasons men abuse women are too numerous to mention in this book. However, I'll mention just a few by saying that sin manifests itself in many ways in all our lives.

Apart from Christ, humanity at its best is barely able to keep from self-destructing. Evidence of the depravity of man will only worsen as people continue choosing to live in disobedience to Christ in unhealthy, unwise, and unholy relationships. Terms like *chastity, sexual purity, fidelity*, and *faithfulness* are no longer part of the vocabulary or character of many men and women. The number of children growing up in America without a father in the home is staggering. The number of women letting men who are not their husbands into their bedrooms is just as staggering. The consequences of promiscuous behavior is that America now has a generation of children who don't have a clue what a healthy family is supposed to look like. A generation of angry, confused, and lonely kids, who have been robbed of decent role models in their lives, enter adolescence and adulthood every day across our nation. Few have even the slightest idea what God requires with respect to how a man is to treat a woman. "If Dad can have his girlfriend sleep over for the night, why can't I? If Dad can slap his girlfriend or his wife around, why can't I? If it feels good, I'm going to do it! If it feels bad, I'm going to take it out on someone else." I believe violence against women is going to get much worse in the years to come. Whether you like it or not, there is a universal principle of sowing and reaping that is going to make our people pay a very high price for our rebellion against God and His commandments.

Then, some men just never grow up and continue to act like the spoiled brats they were when they were children. They're immature little boys in men's bodies. Other men who had dysfunctional childhoods have tremendous fear and pain masked in anger, control, abuse, and criminal acts. Controlling and abusing others is as cathartic for some men as an addiction to drugs or alcohol. Still others enter adulthood as good-for-nothing bums who continually use one woman after another, and when one doesn't feel or look good any longer, she's dumped. On to the next one who has her guard down.

Battering works! Men batter and abuse because it works. Terrorized by the abuser, the victim will do anything to keep from getting injured or killed, and the abuser knows it and likes it that way.

Battering is a choice. The abuser chooses to use violence to maintain power and control. He quickly learns which tactics are most effective, and then he uses them very skillfully.

Battering is a learned behavior. It's learned from childhood, school, peers, sports, and the media through observation and rein-forcement. Sunday afternoons and evenings are the worst times of the week for victims of domestic violence and the police officers who are dispatched to the calls for help. Men sit around at home and in bars, drinking all afternoon until they are thoroughly intoxicated. When their favorite sports team loses, they usually take it out on their spouse or children.

Battering is not caused by anger, and less than 5% of domestic violence is related to an illness-based disorder.

Battering is not caused by alcohol, but batterers often use alcohol as an excuse for their behavior. However, alcohol can make a violent person even more violent.

Battering is not caused by out-of-control behavior. The violence is usually controlled and directed only toward family members. Batterers make choices about whom they will abuse, what they will do to their victim, and when and where it will happen.

Battering is not caused by the victim's behavior. The batterer focuses on the victim's behavior in order to shift blame and responsibility for his own actions.

Manipulation

Batterers are very adept at manipulating the police, and unless a police officer is trained to know what to look for he probably won't recognize the tactics being employed on him. The first thing a batterer wants to do is to connect with the officer at some basic level. It's not uncommon for the batterer to greet the officers at the front door or to be waiting in the driveway when they arrive. He may greet them with a smile and a handshake and say something like, "I'm so glad you guys are here, she's out of control again," or "I'm not sure what's wrong with her but I think she's off her medication again." At various times while the officers are trying to figure out what happened, the batterer might say something like, "She gets nuts like this about once a month during her period. You know what they're like, don't you, officer?" Batterers will also attempt to see if he and the officer have common friends or common interests. "I think I know your brother Frank down at the bowling alley," or "I know you're just doing your job, officer. In fact, I thought about being a cop once but then I realized what a tough job you guys have."

In order to gain credibility with the officers on the scene, the batterer will conform his personality to suit what he believes are the expectations of the officers. If the police have been to the house more than once, the batterer probably knows the officers by their first names and will address them that way. I know of a very wealthy businessman in our county who has gone to such extremes to influence the police that he has dropped off gourmet donuts and cookies at the police station. He clipped thank-you notes on the box, expressing gratitude to the officers for their help in controlling his wife. He even went so far as to invite the officers to his mansion for social gatherings. His wife Angela allowed me to use her testimony for this book—you will read it in chapter ten. This particular police department would benefit from some much-needed and long-overdue domestic violence training.

The goal of the batterer is to get the victim arrested just once. If that happens, the batterer just keeps reminding the police every time they arrive that the victim was arrested before for domestic violence.

From that point on, her credibility is nearly zero. The batterer grows stronger and the victim grows weaker. When an innocent victim is arrested, the shock, fear, and shame she experiences are often so great that she will never call the police again.

Once an innocent victim has been arrested and later returns to the abuser, all the abuser has to do to maintain control over her from that time on is simply threaten to call the police and have her arrested again.

Police officers also need to watch for cross complaints. If the batterer senses that he may be the one getting arrested, he will begin to make all kinds of false allegations like, "She threatened to kill me," or "She had a knife in her hand before you arrived, officer." Internally, the abuser is thinking, "If I'm going to jail, she's going, too." Cross complaints are usually exaggerated, designed to get even with the victim and confuse the officer.

Not long ago I learned of a batterer in my jurisdiction who called the police from a location other than his house and then met them at a local restaurant. He cleverly convinced them that his wife was drunk, out of control, and that she had threatened to kill him. The police, believing his story and now biased, accompanied him back to the house. Despite her pleas to be heard, they threatened to lock up the woman if they got another call from her husband. Then they wrote a report indicating that she was the problem. If they had checked National Crime Information Center records, they would have found that her husband had been arrested previously for armed robbery, interstate prostitution, and domestic violence. Police officers must take the time to do a thorough investigation at each domestic violence call.

Stalkers

There are three types of stalkers, and all are potentially dangerous. Stalking behavior is extremely prevalent in battering relationships and is an important indicator of the dangerousness of the batterer. If the batterer cannot envision life without the victim, or if the separation causes him great despair or rage, the batterer may choose to kill. This is usually where stalking begins because it puts the batterer back in control again.

The domestic stalker is the type of stalker that police most often have contact with. He spends time gathering intelligence on his victim— finding out where she lives and works, what time she gets off, and who she's dating. He harasses her friends, family, and coworkers for information. He follows the victim, makes anonymous phone calls, and leaves notes, flowers, and gifts on her car or at her door. He damages her property, kills her pets, breaks into her house, and watches her sleep. The domestic stalker believes that a tortured relationship is better than no relationship at all. He is easily stressed out and has usually experienced an abusive childhood. Additionally, he exhibits a macho exterior to hide feelings of inferiority and has a history of abusing women.

The narcissistic stalker is more dangerous than the domestic stalker. His sense of self is very fragile and he becomes easily enraged with insult or criticism. When rejected, he tries to destroy his victim's reputation, family, or life. Several years ago a female television anchor in a major media market broke up with her boyfriend, who turned out to be a narcissistic stalker. Over the next several weeks he flooded the television station with hundreds of fax and email letters, telling her coworkers that she was a drug user and a prostitute. He nearly destroyed her career.

The erotomaniac stalker maintains an over-idealized view of romance and is disturbed at a very deep level. He maintains an intense devotion to the victim and believes they have perfect love. He believes that he and his victim are wrought by destiny and nothing can break their union. He is convinced that the victim is in love with him but cannot return the love because the victim is stuck in a relationship with someone else. Oftentimes the stalker and victim have never met.

The three occupations that batterers are commonly drawn to are law enforcement, clergy, and the military.

Police officers are expected and paid to control people on every call they are sent to. If they lose control of anyone or anything even for a moment, they may end up dead. If you want to live very long on the street, you must learn how to control people quickly with looks, language, negotiating skills, posture, threats, and force. Most police officers learn how to turn off the control portion of their personality before they go home. The ones who don't learn this important skill end up with family disturbances and are in one relational mess after another.

To some extent, all pastors have to exert control over staff, volunteers, and people trying to divide the church over various issues. Most of that control is reasonable and comes in the form of directed guidance—it is simply a matter of helping people understand his vision and the need for unity. However, all around the country there are far too many instances of sexual abuse by clergy of women and children in counseling. There are too many instances of pastors physically assaulting their wives and children. Pastors have tremendous power and control.

Many abusers meet their victims in church because they know the church will reinforce the belief that women must remain with an abuser. In a study of court-ordered anger treatment programs, evangelical pastors were the worst to treat because of entrenched thinking. They believed they were entitled to batter and control. They also wrote letters and made calls on behalf of batterers in their congregations more often than others supporting the batterer. Statistics show about two out of ten pastors changed as a result of the anger treatment program.

The military can also be a haven for batterers and those who control. Soldiers are required to "conquer" nations and take enemies captive. If they lose control, they lose the war. Soldiers are trained to be submissive only to their own chain of command. If a ranking officer tells a subordinate to charge up a hill into enemy gunfire, he must— or face the consequences. Military life can be very difficult for women, and family violence occurs frequently. When highly trained, highly motivated soldiers go out on the town for a night and come home to a wife who doesn't want anything to do with a drunken husband, anything can, and often does, happen.

Remember, the only thing more dangerous than a human being is a human being in crisis. Batterers are dangerous and need to be dealt with appropriately by law enforcement. Victims need to put distance between themselves and the abuser as soon as it is safe to get away.

CHAPTER *3*

Profile of
the Abused

Like the abusers, the abused come in every race, age, sex, economic level, profession, and religious background. There are many reasons why a woman stays in a battering relationship. People who have never had to endure physical or emotional abuse oftentimes ask the victim, "Why did you stay; why didn't you just get out?" Sometimes the question is asked out of curiosity, though at other times it is spoken with an undercurrent of disbelief (i.e., "It couldn't have been that bad, you must have liked it," or "If you really wanted to leave, you would have left"). Sometimes people look at the abused and see them as weak, indecisive, and somehow partially responsible for their predicament because they don't have the strength to leave the abuser. In fact just the opposite is true. Victims are very strong people because they have had to learn how to survive and cope with the abuser.

Let's look at some of the many factors that keep women trapped in abusive relationships. When a woman considers leaving her abuser, she must think about some or all of the following:

She faces heightened danger. Most people think that if she just left, the abuse would end. This is often not the case. Physical abuse, stalking, and harassment may continue for years after separation. In fact, immediately after leaving is the most dangerous time for a woman. She is 75% more likely to be killed when she attempts to report abuse or to leave an abusive relationship.

She fears economic hardship and lacks alternative housing. Many women are economically dependent on the male partner. Whether out of necessity for her to care for the children or because he won't let her work (a controlling tactic), she faces poverty if she leaves. In the first year of divorce, a woman's standard of living drops by 73% and a man's improves by an average of 42%. Finding housing is difficult, and homelessness is a real possibility. Up to 50% of all homeless women and children in this country are fleeing domestic violence.

Poverty is the most critical economic problem facing older women today. Unmarried older women are at particularly high risk for poverty in old age. The fear of being poor and alone can keep an older woman in an abusive relationship. Many times older women are met with a great deal of guilt and resentment from their adult children. It is often difficult for children to accept the fact that their mother has made a decision independent of what their father may need. Often they do not support their mother's decision to leave in order to end the violence and find some level of safety and freedom. A mother who supported her children all their young lives now looks to them as adults for moral support only to find there is none. As a result, many older women remain in abusive relationships.

She thinks she should stay for the sake of the children. Some women believe that it is truly better for the children to be raised with both parents present, especially if the abuser has not physically harmed the children. However, some abusers threaten to harm or take the children, and the mother has every reason to believe his threats. More than

50% of child abductions result from domestic violence, most of which are perpetrated by the fathers.

She thinks she has no place to go. Economic dependence, lack of self-confidence, and lack of a place to go are major reasons a woman stays in an abusive relationship. She may be unaware of domestic violence shelters or may not have access to them because she is isolated, illiterate, has a medical condition, or has other debilitating problems. She may not even realize that domestic violence is a crime. Many times in an abusive relationship the husband will decide who his wife will associate with, make her get permission before she goes anywhere, and impose strict financial restraints on her to prevent her from having any sense of financial independence. In order to keep her silent regarding the abuse, he will make all major decisions for her on a daily basis. Before long the woman begins to feel that she has no life of her own and is nothing more than a robot for her abusive spouse. She begins to believe that even if she did speak up, no one would listen to her.

She loves him, and just wants the violence to stop. She may love the abuser and remembers the "good times" before the violence started, or she may think about his loving gestures during the honeymoon stage. She may feel that she can help him change or that if she just tries harder, the abuse will stop. She may think she causes the violence. Over a period of time she begins to believe that she is responsible for her husband's anger and begins to ask herself, "What am I doing wrong? Am I causing all the problems in our marriage?"

She has difficulty trusting people. An abused wife feels terribly betrayed. The relationship has not turned out as she envisioned. Even though there may have been some indications before the marriage that her spouse overreacted in certain situations, she never dreamed he would someday turn his wrath on her. In the early days of a new marriage, the husband usually lavishes his new bride with much affection and attention. This is the very thing she found most appealing in her mate. However, under the romantic mask lurked the monster of control and abuse. Eventually she comes to the realization that her "knight in shining armor" is really a nightmare armed with powerful forces to control and possess. Finally this woman realizes the deception her mate has employed against her, and the reality that she is married to a controlling and abusive man settles in. As a result, many abused women have difficulty trusting anyone, especially men who are in a position of authority such as a pastor, police officer, or father.

The woman feels powerless. An aggressive husband's tactics of intimidation, threats, mind games, and violence, along with his economic restrictions, oftentimes leave a wife feeling that she is incapable of stopping the abuse, so she surrenders to the abuser's will. Her sense of being overwhelmed by a superior force leaves her feeling that she can't end the abuse and the pain it has caused her and the children.

She has lost her feeling of her self-worth. A woman who has her self-worth attacked day after day eventually comes to a point where she begins to believe that she is worthless, stupid, and deserving of being abused. She is constantly reminded that she can't make it on her own, think for herself, understand or solve simple problems, or cope with life's demands. Her feelings, hopes, dreams, and desires count for nothing. Her only goal is to survive from one beating to the next. The woman begins to lose sight of her significance as a wife, mother, and person, and she begins to view herself as a failure.

She fears rejection by the church and God. Many women stay with an abuser because the church has mistakenly taught them that a woman cannot leave her husband except for marital infidelity. That's simply not true. That information has been given by pastors all over America who may have been more concerned about what the breakup of another marriage would look like to their congregation than what was happening to the wife who was getting the daylights beaten out of her. Far too many women have been told to go back home, develop a submissive spirit, and pray harder for God to give them patience. The fact is that some of them went back to their deaths! Some of the very pastors who gave this advice were abusing their own wives at the same time. After 10 or 15 years of unrelenting abuse, most women don't want to hear a homily on submission. It may have worked for some, but not for them; their husbands are as cruel as ever. The abuse that is heaped on them is privately administered and privately endured. Many women have stayed with abusive husbands and needlessly endured decades of physical and emotional abuse out of fear of being rejected by their church and condemned by God. Many have been betrayed by every male authority figure in their lives—father, husband, police officers, and pastors.

She faces the unrelenting pursuit of the batterer. When the batterer is faced with the loss of the victim to law enforcement intervention or legal separation, he will often turn his attention to getting the victim back. He may use a combination of kindness and cruelty to wear her down and convince her to return.

She fears what the batterer might do. The victim is afraid that the batterer may take out his rage on her family, children, friends, coworkers, pets, or property. There may have been very credible threats of homicide or suicide. Some victims would rather live with or have casual contact with a batterer than to completely separate. This arrangement provides her with daily knowledge of his moods and whereabouts, and it allows the victim to gauge whether or not danger is near. Otherwise she must guess at what strategies to employ to stay safe. This gives her a sense of control over her daily life as well.

Behaviors

Battered women often display a broad range of behavior when police officers are called to intervene. It is not uncommon for a woman to suddenly see a power shift in her favor after the cavalry shows up and attack her abuser right in front of the police. For years she may have felt powerless to react to his torment, and when she finally feels like she's got some muscle on her side, she explodes with anger.

Statistics show women use violence in about 50% of all domestic violence calls, but only about 5% are the primary or predominant physical aggressor. I'll talk more about the term "predominant physical aggressor" and a woman's right to self-defense in chapter seven. Women use violence in marriage relationships and can be abusive, but rape, intimidation, or coercion rarely accompany their violence the way they do with men. Physical violence is not an effective tool for women because of physical size and strength differences. There are times when women should be arrested for violent behavior that is retaliatory. Police officers must be able to distinguish between retaliation and a legitimate claim of self-defense by doing a thorough interview with everyone involved and by a close examination of both offensive and defensive wounds found on both the batterer and victim.

Hostility Toward the Police

The victim may become uncooperative and hostile toward the police because she may not want her assailant arrested—she just wants the violence to stop. She may also fear retribution from the abuser if he is arrested and later released from jail. Or she may be afraid that an arrest might cost the abuser the loss of his job or career. Finally, she may have called the police in the past and nothing happened. They may have failed to act, or the prosecutor or the courts did nothing for her and she lacks confidence in the criminal justice system. Police officers should be prepared to encounter a wide range of responses from victims such as hurt, anger, intoxication, hostility, confusion, hysteria, depression, shame, embarrassment, and denial that anything is wrong.

The average domestic violence victim is assaulted seven times before she ever calls the police, and she usually does not make a decision to leave the batterer until the police have responded 7–11 times. The repeated calls for help from the victim frustrate police officers who do not understand the dynamics of domestic violence. They often become angry when the victim refuses to leave the abuser, fails to cooperate, or allows the abuser to move back in after he's been arrested.

When Violence Begins at Home by K. J. Wilson, and *Battered Into Submission: The Tragedy of Wife Abuse in the Christian Home* by James and Phyllis Alsdurf are essential tools for pastors, counselors, and anyone touched by the consequences of wife abuse.

Confronting the Myths

There are several myths surrounding the issue of wife abuse. Let's look at four of them.

Myth #1: Some men can't help themselves. Some believe that there are men who don't have the ability to cope with frustration. It's said that these men have no choice but to abuse. In response to this claim, James and Phyllis Alsdurf state in *Battered Into Submission,* "If frustrating situations offered only one option, abusers would be equally violent on the job, driving in traffic, or interacting with friends; but that is simply not true. The majority of abusers direct their violence specifically and purposely toward their wives." Additionally, this is a dangerous view to hold because it allows the abuser to dodge responsibility for his actions. Failure to hold abusers responsible only adds fuel to a fire burning out of control.

Myth #2: Alcohol is the problem. While alcohol and other drugs are factors in many abusive marriages, in others they are not. It is wrong to assume that alcohol or drugs is the fundamental cause of spouse abuse. Chemical dependencies often inflame and complicate abusive relationships, but they are only part of the problem. Removing alcohol, for instance, still leaves the heart and the root of the abuse unexposed and unchallenged.

Myth #3: Abused women have themselves to blame. Some believe that wife abuse would not occur if it were not for women who drive their husbands over the edge. They point out that some women "bait" their husbands into abusing them with a frigid attitude or constant nagging. They maintain that some women actually "buy" the attention and sympathy of others by provoking their husbands to violence.

While there may be occasions when this kind of baiting exists, it is rare. It's a well-known fact that battered women generally keep the abuse private. That's why wife battering is commonly referred to as the "silent crime." Battered women normally don't seek sympathy from others. They keep it to themselves because of the shame they feel, and because they're afraid of what might happen if they report their husbands' behavior.

Some wives admit to provoking their husbands' rage, not because they like being abused but because they have been through the cycle enough times to know that after the storm their husbands are inclined to be remorseful, kind, and gentle. Additionally, "getting the abuse over with" eases the enormous fear of wondering if the storm is about to strike. For many abused wives, living with the overwhelming fear of not knowing when the abuse will happen again is worse than the abusive incident itself.

In some marriages, the wife is more verbal than her husband. She can out-maneuver him in an argument, give him reason to feel weak and incompetent, and sometimes provoke him to anger. When he finally blows up, her moral superiority and low opinion of him appear to be confirmed. He feels even lower about himself, while she, at considerable cost to herself, appears to be vindicated.

Again, while such relationships exist, they do not prove that a woman is to blame for being abused. No one should ever be blamed for another's abusive behavior.

Myth #4: The Bible does not permit women to report an abusive husband. This is probably the most serious of all myths because so many battered women have been encouraged to silently apply the "submissive wife" principle of 1 Peter 3:1–6. So many well-meaning pastors and counselors have sent wives back into abusive homes after quoting the apostle Peter's words.

> "Wives, in the same way be submissive to your husbands so that, if any of them do not believe the word, they may be won over without words by the behavior of their wives, when they see the purity and reverence of your lives. Your beauty should not come from outward adornment, such as braided hair and the wearing of gold jewelry and fine clothes. Instead, it should be that of your inner self, the unfading beauty of a gentle and quiet spirit, which is of great worth in God's sight. For this is the way the holy women of the past who put their hope in God used to

make themselves beautiful. They were submissive to their own husbands, like Sarah, who obeyed Abraham and called him master. You are her daughters if you do what is right and do not give way to fear." (NIV)

Then in verse 7, Peter went on to say to husbands:

"Husbands, in the same way be considerate as you live with your wives, and treat them with respect as the weaker partner and as heirs with you of the gracious gift of life, so that nothing will hinder your prayers." (NIV)

These clear words and timeless principles are often misapplied in abuse situations for several reasons:

Differences of culture. In his commentary on 1 Peter, William Barclay explains, "It may seem strange that Peter's advice to wives is six times as long as advice to husbands. That was because the wife's problem was far more difficult than that of the husband. If a husband became a Christian, he would automatically bring his wife with him into the church, and there would be no problem. But if a wife became a Christian, while her husband did not, she had taken a step which in the ancient world was unprecedented, and which produced the acutest problems." Barclay then goes on to describe the lack of legal protection offered to women in the first century.

First century women and slaves could not appeal to 20th century assault and battery laws. An endangered woman did not have the option of calling 911, an abuse hotline, or the local police. In our day, we can call upon the provisions of government and law enforcement. If the husband is a believer, and his abuse has not escalated to criminal proportions, a woman can appeal to the principles of Matthew 18:15–17 and ask the church to intervene on her behalf.

When an abused woman asks the church for help, it is important to remember that the God of the Bible has always asked people of strength to come to the assistance of those who are weak and oppressed

(Ezekiel 34:4). Godly people must not send a battered woman back to her home with the advice to "be more submissive." They need to do everything possible to provide whatever legal, social, or spiritual protection is available. When appropriate, they must help a battered woman to apply the full extent of the law. Their motive must not be to return evil for evil, but to use the principle of government to bring an out-of-control husband to his senses. No one does an abusive husband a favor by allowing him to continue degrading himself and his wife with violence.

The nature of godly submission. The woman who passively allows her husband to abuse her may be sincerely trying to be obedient to the principles of 1 Peter 3:1–6. Or she might be bearing her trauma silently in the belief that to report the abuse would result in even greater endangerment. In either case, it needs to be noted that Peter was asking women for a specific kind of submission. In the following pages, we will see that he was calling for the kind of godly submission that invites a husband to be the servant-leader God made him to be. Peter's intent was not to help abusive husbands indulge in the childish lust for power and control that Jesus condemned (Mark 10:42–45; 1 Peter 3:7).

The example of Christ. The immediate context of 1 Peter 3:1–7 says that we must be willing to suffer as Christ suffered for us. Peter reminded us that Jesus suffered unfair treatment without returning insult for insult or evil for evil. This may sound like a reason for not reporting or opposing an abusive husband. But think about how Christ suffered for us. Jesus was first of all submissive to His Father in heaven. His submission was always controlled by what brought honor to God and help to others. He was willing to suffer. But His suffering was for doing good, for seeking the life and well-being of others—Jesus wasn't indulging the evil actions of His enemies and submitting to their selfish whims.

For those reasons and others, I believe that it is a dangerous myth that Christian women must not oppose abusive husbands. Applying 1 Peter 3:1–6 in this way, however, requires a woman to think carefully about why and how she is living out the kind of submission Peter was calling for.

There are many women who have really never experienced genuine love. Erotic passions or physical arousal they may have experienced is often perceived as love. Love is not a feeling. Love is not lust. Feelings come and go as time passes. In most marriages, feelings of warmth and affection will come and go with time and circumstance, changes in health, age, and other factors. Love is a commitment to one another that says, "I accept you as you are...as my equal...for the rest of my life, even when I don't feel like I love you." Here's how God described love through the writings of the apostle Paul.

> "Love is patient, love is kind and is not jealous; love does not brag and is not arrogant, does not act unbecomingly; it does not seek its own, is not provoked, does not take into account a wrong suffered, does not rejoice in unrighteousness, but rejoices with the truth; bears all things, believes all things, hopes in all things, endures all things. Love never fails."
>
> —1 Corinthians 13:4–8

If only men would learn to love their wives by this standard, most of the violence in the family unit would stop. There isn't a woman anywhere who would not welcome and respond to this kind of love. Dear friend, if you have been battered and abused for part or all of your life, it is quite possible that you have never really experienced what true love is. Love never fails. This is the kind of love God intended for you to experience and still wants for you.

> "A new commandment I give to you, that you love one another."
>
> —John 13:34

CHAPTER *4*

The Effects of
Domestic Violence
on Children

This is a subject that cannot be adequately covered in just one chapter of a book. Child psychologists and other mental health care professionals have written entire volumes on this aspect of family violence in far greater depth than I can. As hard as I try to cover what I believe are some of the most important points of this tragic subject, I'm sure I will miss many important ones. Before we begin to look at the effects of violence on children, let me extend this warning to you.

If your children or the children of a person with whom you reside are being battered and abused and you know it, and you do nothing to stop it, you may be arrested. In many states across the U.S., laws have been passed that hold another person criminally responsible for failing to act on behalf of a child. You could be charged with being "party to a crime" for standing by and doing nothing. If your children are in danger, get them out of that environment the minute it is safe to do so, and report the abuser to a child protection agency, the police, or social services.

Risks to Children

Children in violent homes face three risks: (1) The risk of observing traumatic events, (2) the risk of being abused, and (3) the risk of being neglected.

More than one-half of the children whose mothers are abused are likely to be victims of physical abuse also. Older children are often injured while trying to protect their mothers. Whether or not the children are abused physically, they suffer emotional trauma and psychological scars from watching their father beat their mother. Children have a built-in tape recorder running in their brain, and data is being stored on that tape every minute of every day. Stored memory, when recalled, stimulates emotions associated with that positive or negative memory.

My maternal grandfather passed away before I was born, and my grandmother re-married. The man she married routinely beat her up. After 40 years, I can still remember seeing her with black eyes, a swollen face, and bruised arms. Even though Grandma never said anything to me, I knew what was going on. I'd find knives hidden in odd places in her house, and eventually I found out that she had put them there as a last resort for self-defense in case she ever got to the point where she felt her husband was going to kill her.

In homes where domestic violence occurs, fear, instability, and confusion replace the love, comfort, and nurturing that children need. These children live in constant fear of physical harm from the person who is supposed to care for them. They may feel guilt at loving the abuser or they may blame themselves for causing the violence.

Such children may experience stress-related physical ailments, hearing and speech problems, higher risks of alcohol/drug abuse, and juvenile delinquency. Many children who witness domestic violence are also victims of physical abuse themselves. Each year an estimated 3.3

million children witness domestic violence.

A major study of more than 900 children at battered women's shelters found that nearly 70% of the children were themselves victims of physical abuse. Some 5% had been hospitalized because of the abuse. However, only 20% had been identified and served by Child Protective Services prior to coming to the shelter. The same study found that the male batterer most often abused the children. In about one-fourth of the cases, both parents abused the children—in a few instances, only the mother.

Studies show that mothers are eight times more likely to batter their children if they're in an abusive environment than if they are safe.

In homes where domestic violence occurs, children may indirectly receive injuries. They may be hurt when household items are thrown or weapons are used. Infants may be injured if they are being held by their mother when the batterer strikes out.

Approximately 90% of children are aware of the violence directed at their mother.

Children are present in 41-55% of homes where police are called to intervene in domestic violence calls. I have many vivid memories of responding to calls where a mother and father had been fighting. The children were already terrified before the police arrived because of what they had seen and heard. Then they watched in additional horror as we fought with the father, handcuffed him, and hauled him off to jail.

I can still hear the children begging through their tears, "Please, please don't hurt my daddy, don't take my daddy away." As hard as I tried to comfort the children, I was unable to. Nothing I said to them would calm their troubled hearts. The anguish of the children's pleas upset me greatly toward the abuser because of what he had forced me to see and hear. I didn't mind dealing with his violence or his verbal abuse, but I absolutely hated what it did to the kids. As long as those children live, they will never forget the day the big, bad policeman came and took their daddy away to jail.

Some of the emotional effects of domestic violence on children include:
• Taking responsibility for the abuse

- Constant anxiety (that another abuse will occur)
- Guilt for not being able to stop the abuse or for loving the abuser
- Fear of abandonment
- Depression
- Low self-esteem
- Isolation and loneliness because they are afraid to tell anyone
- Being starved for tender affection and peace of mind

The following are some of the tactics parents use on children who are caught in the middle of divorce or domestic violence:
- The child is beaten by the father during visitation and sent back to the mother as a sign of what might happen to her.
- One parent brainwashes the child into believing that he/she has been sexually abused by the other during visitation.
- One parent tells the child that the other parent doesn't want them around because they interfere with mommy's or daddy's new roommate.

The documented reactions of children between birth and five years of age who have been exposed to violence in their homes included sleep disturbances, bedwetting, separation anxiety, and failure to thrive. Children 6–12 years old exhibited eating disorders, seductive or manipulative behavior, fears of abandonment, or loss of control. Adolescents tended to run away, become pregnant, experience suicidal or homicidal thoughts, or engage in drug or alcohol abuse.

Women who are victims of domestic violence may neglect their children for a number of reasons. They may give full attention to the abusive partner in an effort to appease and control the level of violence, or they may be unresponsive to children due to their own fears.

At other times a battered mother may be so fearful of the abuser focusing his anger on the children that she will over-discipline them in an effort to control the children's behavior and protect them from what she perceives as greater abuse.

Children who are neglected because of domestic violence may show signs of listlessness and developmental delay. Behavioral problems may include begging for or stealing food, eating inappropriate objects, erratic school attendance, poor social relationships with peers, and delinquent acts such as vandalism, drug use, and drinking.

While witnessing abuse may at times be the same as psychological abuse of the child, this is not the case for many children in such circumstances. Many women, in spite of being abused themselves, do attend to the psychological needs of their children.

The Influence of Parents

Perhaps the greatest damage done to a child who has witnessed domestic violence or has suffered abuse at the hands of a father is that he/she interprets who God is through the words and actions of that father. Their earthly father directly shapes their perception of a heavenly father. If the biological father is mean-spirited, violent, uncaring, unpredictable, cold, absent, and gives love and affirmation based on performance, then God is viewed the same way. If a father is patient, kind, gentle, tenderhearted, and encouraging, then God is viewed in that way. It is much easier for a child to accept and trust Christ as his Savior when he views God as loving and caring. That is one of the reasons why Paul wrote in Colossians 3:21: "Fathers, do not exasperate your children, so that they may not lose heart."

I am convinced that we are greatly influenced by three factors: (1) our genetics, (2) the parenting we received, and (3) the choices we make.

We can't do anything about our genetics. For example, in a set of fraternal twins, one child may be very passive, obedient, calm, and easy to raise, while the other is very strong willed, defiant, and into every kind of mischief there is.

Our parents pass values on to us that greatly influence the choices we make. The choices we make are going to be greatly influenced by the values passed down to us by our parents for either good or bad. That's not to say that many wonderful parents who did nearly everything right in raising a child are somehow responsible for a child who grows up and robs a bank. Likewise, many children who grew up in terrible environments have also gone on to become pillars of the community.

I am absolutely convinced of the biblical mandate in Proverbs 22:6, which says: "Train up a child in the way he should go, even when he is old he will not depart from it."

After spending many hours dealing with gang members and juvenile delinquents, I developed the following guidelines to help ensure the success or failure of a child. If you choose to parent your child by applying the principles found in the formula for "Building a Foundation for Your Child's Success," there is a high probability your child will enter his/her adult life with a solid foundation. That foundation will become the launching pad upon which future decisions will be made. If you choose to parent your child using the formula guaranteeing failure, then I can almost assure you that your child's life will have counted for nothing, and he/she will be another warm body in a prison cell somewhere. If you love your children, you will not subject them to abuse. If you love them, you will remove them from a violent or abusive environment and make whatever sacrifices are needed to ensure they have a chance to grow up safe and reasonably well adjusted.

A Foundation for Your Child's Failure

Here are some fail-safe ways to make sure your children will struggle in life and rarely experience success.

• Ignore your child and let him/her run free without boundaries, supervision, or accountability.

• Discipline your children in anger or not all. Run your home in a dictatorial manner. Refuse to be tolerant or flexible. Allow no room for mistakes.

• Be your child's best friend. Never do anything to upset him/her, and fulfill their every demand.

• Don't ask or expect them to do household chores.

• Allow them to listen to any kind of music or video they desire, even if it's violent or racist.

- Tolerate disrespect and back talk. Let them call you by your first name.
- Husbands and wives, tear each other down in front of the children. Men, belittle and tease your wife and show the kids how stupid their mother really is.
- Never praise your child for their accomplishments or affirm their worth to the family.
- Make them feel uncomfortable talking about sex and other sensitive issues.
- Constantly criticize and find fault.
- Keep bringing up past failures.
- Make your children believe that no matter how hard they try, they can't ever be good enough for you.
- Let them know you don't trust them.
- Spend little or no time with them.
- Break your promises.
- Never go to church, tear down the government the way you tear down your spouse, and do nothing to build character in them.
- Let them get away with lying, cheating, stealing, etc.
- Stand up for your children even when you know they are wrong. Tear down the teacher and the police like you do to your spouse when they try to hold your child accountable for his/her bad behavior.
- Make your career and the pursuit of money the most important thing in life.
- Ignore the warning signs of his/her bad behavior. Say, "they're just going through a stage."
- Abuse your children physically, sexually, or emotionally.
- Attack your daughter's femininity and your son's masculinity by referring to your son as a sissy boy and to your daughter as cheap.

Building a Foundation for Your Child's Success

On the other hand, there are some tried-and-true ways for building a foundation for your child that will lead to their happiness and eventual success.

- Men, show the kids how much you love and respect their mother. Let them know that they cannot get away with ignoring her directives or showing disrespect for her.
- Plan special times alone with each child as well as with the whole family.
- Worship together as a family in your church, and then live out your faith in tangible ways that the kids can see in your actions and hear in your speech. Tell them of God's love, mercy, grace, and forgiveness. Tell them about eternity and the consequences of rejecting Jesus. Tell them there is a heaven and a hell. Tell them there is a devil and how he operates. Teach them the Ten Commandments.
- Forgive one another quickly when mistakes are made. Keep short lists of wrongs. Don't let the sun go down on your anger. Resolve the conflict quickly and gently.
- Make your children a high priority and praise them often. Tell your daughters how beautiful they are and affirm their femininity. Give lots of hugs. Tell your sons how handsome they are and affirm their masculinity.
- Set high but reasonable standards of excellence for your kids, and guide them toward goals in sports, music, or academics.
- When your kids are wrong, hold them accountable. Or at the very least, let the police or the school hold them accountable without interference from you.
- When you are wrong, admit it.
- When you have been wrong in dealing with your children, tell them you're sorry and ask for their forgiveness.
- Never discipline your child in anger. When you do punish, let the punishment fit the offense.
- Don't be cruel or excessive. Remember, you were a kid once yourself.
- Let your kids know that no matter what, your love for them is unconditional and that they are more valuable to you than your career or your golfing buddies.

- Create an environment in your home where your kids feel comfortable talking about sex and drugs.
- Teach them about the consequences of breaking God's laws.
- Don't drag up past failures. Heap loads of praise on each one, and be a constant source of encouragement to them.
- Establish reasonable boundaries in the areas of dating, music, art, behavior, language, and dress. Even though kids won't admit it, they will know you love them if you set limits in their life.

There came a point in each one of my children's lives during their teenage years that I had to let them know that I wasn't their friend—I was their dad. And because I was their dad and would someday stand before Almighty God to give an account for the way I raised them, I was going to make tough choices for them and set guidelines. They didn't like it at the time, but they understand it now. Don't be afraid to be a parent. You can be your child's buddy when they are old enough, and no longer need you to parent them that way.

CHAPTER 5

Understanding Your Worth as a Woman

"Because of the tender mercy of our God, with which the Sunrise from on high will visit us, to shine upon those who sit in darkness and the shadow of death, to guide our feet into the way of peace."

—Luke 1:78–79

When I think of Jesus referred to as the Sunrise from on high, I can't help but think of several times in my life when the night seemed so dark, so empty, so lonely that I wondered if I'd make it till dawn. But when morning came, I saw the sunrise and was drawn to its warmth and light, believing that the new day would bring relief from the terrible darkness. Oh, what a difference a sunrise can make!

Women loved everything there was to love about Jesus. They were drawn to Him like to a beautiful morning sunrise, basking in His warmth and unconditional love. They felt so safe when they were near Him because Jesus saw them through eyes of perfect purity and love. Unlike many men who see women as sex objects to be used, controlled, manipulated, or exploited, He affirmed their worth and never degraded them. He spoke to them with understanding and patience. He enjoyed being with women, and they enjoyed talking and listening to Him, eating with Him, and oftentimes traveling with Him. Jesus was absolutely comfortable around women, and they loved and adored Him because He enabled them to understand how divinely important they were in all of God's creation.

Jesus never responded to women in anger, never attempted to control them, and He never insisted on their allegiance. He served them and treated them with dignity, gentleness, and respect, just as He did everyone else. Jesus never abused women physically, mentally, emotionally, or sexually. He was divinely aware of their needs, reaching out to them with arms of tenderness and affection and with eyes of understanding and love. Jesus modeled God's unconditional love for mankind so man could model that same kind of love. Let's look at how women occupied a very special place in His heart, life, and ministry.

"The scribes and the Pharisees brought a woman caught in adultery, and having set her in the center of the court, they said to Him [Jesus], 'Teacher, this woman has been caught in adultery, in the very act. Now in the Law Moses commanded us to stone such women; what then do You say?' They were saying this, testing Him, so that they might have grounds for accusing Him. But Jesus stooped down and with His finger wrote on the ground. But when they persisted in asking Him, He straightened up, and said to them, 'He who is without sin among you, let him be the first to throw a stone at her.' Again He stooped down and wrote on the ground. When they heard it, they began to go out one by one, beginning with the older ones, and He was left alone, and the woman, where she was, in the center of the court. Straightening up, Jesus said to her, 'Woman, where are they? Did no one condemn you?' She said, 'No one Lord.' And Jesus said, 'I do not condemn you, either. Go. From now on sin no more.'"

—John 8:3–11

Jesus loved this woman unconditionally, saved her life from murderous men, and forgave her sins.

Take a moment to think about this story. It's probable that this woman was dragged to the area where Jesus was. I doubt if she walked there on her own—most likely she fought to break free from the grasp of her abductors to get away. She probably begged and pleaded with her captors because she knew what the prescribed punishment for her behavior would be. She was perhaps terrified and crying uncontrollably, knowing that death was only moments away. People were gathering around, picking up rocks, and yelling, "Kill the harlot." Jesus could just have easily said, "You know what, she deserves everything she's about to get. She knew the law; it's her own fault. Make an example out of her so others will learn." But He didn't. He loved this woman unconditionally, and He knew that her great need was to receive mercy and forgiveness. Jesus calmed the raging storm that was about to overtake this woman's life.

She met Him in terror, but she left with peace in her soul. She came condemned by men, held captive by sin, but left forgiven by the Savior. Jesus' behavior was designed to convict every participant there, showing them that they were all sinners, deserving death. Jesus knew every sin in the heart of every accuser who was there that day, and He could write them out on the ground in front of them. Jesus took pity on the woman, and even though she broke God's law, He extended mercy and forgiveness to her. The message here is God's awareness, mercy, and forgiveness.

Jesus knows the painful stones that men have thrown at you, and He sees the bruises, scars, and cuts they left behind. He also understands the internal struggles of your abuser. He understands you and accepts you just as you are. Whether you're face down in the gutter, dying from AIDS, driving a Porsche in an evening gown, or somewhere in-between, His love is everlasting and unconditional. Come as you are.

Let's take another quick look at what an important role women played in Jesus' life.

The announcement concerning the greatest event in the history of mankind was made to women. The resurrection of Christ was told by an angel, appointed by God, to Mary Magdalene, Mary the mother of James, and Salome when they entered the tomb.

> "And he said to them, 'Do not be amazed; you are look-
> ing for Jesus the Nazarene, who has been crucified. He
> has risen; He is not here; behold, here is the place where
> they laid Him. But go, tell His disciples and Peter, "He is
> going ahead of you to Galilee; there you will see Him, just
> as He told you."'"
>
> —Mark 16:6–7

The first person to see Jesus after His resurrection was a woman named Mary Magdalene.

> "Now after He had risen early on the first day of the week,
> He first appeared to Mary Magdalene, from whom He had
> cast out seven demons."
>
> —Mark 16:9

Jesus could have appeared to His male disciples immediately after He arose from the dead—He loved them just as much—but He chose instead to have an angel tell the women in His life that He was alive. Jesus loved women with a pure, holy, unconditional love—as He does everyone. God dearly loves *you*. Begin to accept it.

Do you feel like the woman caught in adultery? Do you have a rep-utation for being promiscuous, a drunk, a drug addict, or a prostitute? Have you been beaten, abused, neglected, and unloved for some or all of your life? Are you struggling with a load of shame and guilt? Are you living in fear that someone will discover your past?

Maybe you're none of the above. Perhaps you've lived a country club life and are widely accepted as a pillar of the community, but you are emotionally empty, spiritually dead, physically exhausted, or relationally separated from someone you desperately want to love you. Have you been laboring all your life to find your worth? You can be freed from the bonds that keep you from being all that Jesus intended for you to be. Listen to His words from John 8:31–32:

> "So Jesus was saying to those Jews who had believed Him, 'If you continue in My word, then you are truly disciples of Mine; and you will know the truth, and the truth will make you free.'"

Most of us have grown up believing what we were told as children. The information that we believed then often deeply affects how we feel about ourselves and who we are now. We continue to consciously and subconsciously believe that information as adults, even if what we believe is untrue.

Our minds are powerfully imprinted by deeply held beliefs that we have learned through our environment and experiences. Our beliefs produce thoughts and memories about past events. Those recollections produce emotions, and the emotions trigger actions or behaviors that can be either good or bad. If you had the privilege and good fortune to grow up under the guiding hands of loving, caring, well-balanced parents who affirmed your worth, then you probably entered adulthood with fond childhood memories and are reasonably well adjusted. If you were abused and neglected as a child, then you most certainly have some deeply painful memories that may affect the way you view yourself now.

Don't despair. I believe most people bring some emotional baggage from childhood that deeply affects how they view themselves, and that much of it is very destructive. The information that you and I received from parents, playmates, peers, media, and others was slowly absorbed into our minds as we grew up. Over a period of time, we began to believe that our performance or lack of it measured our worth. If we became rich or famous, we would be respected and desirable. If we remained poor, uneducated, or lacked standing, we would be looked upon as not worth knowing or listening to.

Many of us also came to believe that our parents' love was performance-based or conditional. If you were physically beautiful or naturally gifted, you were looked up to, respected, and part of the in-crowd. If you were overweight and unattractive, you were ignored or viciously teased. If everyone had a date for the junior prom and no one asked you to go, your heart was broken and you believed that you were worthless.

I want to spend some time and expose that lie because we have all bought into it to one degree or another. So much of who we think we are is directly tied to what we do, what we have, or whom we married. Nothing could be further from the truth. God's love is unconditional—it's not performance based.

You and I don't have to achieve or perform for God in order to gain His love and total acceptance! I'm going to say it again—*you and I don't have to achieve or perform for God in order to gain His unconditional love and total acceptance.*

I believe this is the heart of the problem when it comes to abuse. A woman who feels totally worthless by her husband's or the world's wretched, ungodly standards is doomed to being controlled and abused for the rest of her life if she continues to think that way. Satan is the father of lies, and he wants you to remain uninformed and in bondage to your flawed thinking and to his deception. God wants you to understand that your worth is found in Him—in Him alone. God loves us even when we don't love ourselves.

Let's examine what you believe about yourself. From where do you derive your sense of self-worth? From…

- the size of your house?
- your net worth?
- the position you or your husband hold in the business world?

- the size of your annual income?
- your academic accomplishments?
- your physical beauty?
- the social circles you move in?
- who your parents were?
- your past accomplishments?

If you derive any portion of your self-worth from any of the above, you are living according to cultural standard, not God's standard. How are you going to feel about yourself if an economic disaster should befall you and your household income is drastically cut? What if you have to go to a lower standard of living and are forced to walk or ride a bus to go anywhere? How are you going to feel about your sense of self worth if the country club doesn't renew your membership because you can't afford to pay the annual membership fee? How will you feel if your husband no longer finds you beautiful and finds a "newer model" instead? If your sense of worth is based on the approval or rejection of others or on anything else, it does not line up with God's Word.

If you have been abused or are abusing yourself, then understanding your worth in Christ is the key to getting well. Many people who have been abused as children continue to allow themselves to be abused as adults because of a poor self-image or low self-esteem. Your lack of self-esteem may have enabled someone in your life to control you in ways you never thought possible.

When people around you speak well of you, does that make you feel good about yourself? Of course it does—we all enjoy hearing a good word spoken about us. But do you find that your sense of worth goes up because of the positive praise? What happens when someone criticizes you for your opinion, ideas, or work? Do you immediately feel devalued, angry, and hurt? Do you want to flee to an isolated place and just cry because you feel so worthless?

If we have our worth tied to the approval or rejection of others, then every time we feel rejected, we either withdraw to prevent further rejection or start looking for approval and love in all the wrong places.

This is where we usually get hurt, and we hurt badly. We are complex beings, capable of building impenetrable walls around ourselves to protect our emotions from further violence when we feel vulnerable. We are usually afraid to take an honest inventory of *who* we are for fear we may find out *what* we are.

Many people come into their teenage and adult years horribly scarred from incest, alcoholic parents, neglect, severe beatings, verbal abuse, domestic violence, and racial or ethnic discrimination.

Tell God the Truth

When was the last time you had an honest conversation with God and really told Him what you think of Him? Have you refrained from telling God how you feel about Him because you're afraid He'll strike you dead? God wants you and me to have a painfully honest conversation with Him about our feelings and disappointments. It's okay to tell God you're disappointed and angry with Him. It's okay to tell God you don't trust Him and don't love Him if that's the way you feel. It's okay to tell God that you feel betrayed by Him and don't understand why He didn't answer your prayers when you were hurting so badly. God is so big that He can take the criticism and still love you. He wants and invites us to honestly confess our feelings to Him. He loves it when we finally get to a point in our lives where we admit we've tried everything else and need Him.

I encourage you to read through the psalms and see how King David poured out his hurt, fear, anger, joy, sorrow, and repentance before God. David was honest before God, and God wants honesty from us when we speak to Him. One of the hardest things to do is admit to God when we feel worthless—and I have told Him that many times in my life. There have been some very painful times in my life when I've struggled with low self-esteem from past failures and missed opportunities—even as a Christian—and I told God so.

Take some time right now and begin to examine how you feel about yourself and God. Ask Him to help you see where your hurt is, how it's manifesting itself, and what it stems from. His Holy Spirit can lead you on a journey of discovery and healing. The revelation may not all come back at once, but if you work at it regularly, with God's help you will gain understanding and wisdom in your quest to discover the source of your pain. He will also guide you to a trusting relationship with Him through His Son, Jesus Christ, if you don't already know Him as Lord and Savior.

Ask God to help you to honestly answer the following questions:

- Am I really content with who I am?
- Do I like the person I'm turning out to be?
- Do I have peace in my life or am I in constant emotional turmoil?
- Do I understand and know that God loves me and that I love Him?
- Do I constantly try to gain the approval of others?
- Have I compromised my standards in order to be accepted by others?
- Am I afraid of what people will think if they know who I really am?
- What or who is the most important thing in my life?
- Do I trust God enough to tell Him my deepest hurts and darkest secrets?

Our intense desire to be loved and accepted often drives us into career choices and relationships that are not well-suited for us, and we end up in disastrous consequences. Many people who are struggling with low self-esteem and deep, unhealed hurts will do almost anything to gain approval and acceptance, including dating and marrying an abuser. We settle for the worst, when in fact, if we just trusted God in these areas, He would provide us with the best.

The abuser and the abused come to the relationship looking for love and believing that the other is going to fill the void in their lives. It usually doesn't take long for one or both to find out that they don't satisfy one another and their needs are not being met. Soon the verbal attacks start, and the abuser attempts to force the abused to comply with his demands because his needs are not being met. The need to control is a powerful one that can be satisfied only by the complete submission of the abused. When submission no longer satisfies the abuser, he will often escalate the conflict to the physical level, leaving him frustrated and empty after he has battered his victim.

The cataclysmic consequences of Adam's and Eve's sin in the Garden of Eden still take their toll on all of mankind every second of every day. The void that every human being seeks to fill can only be properly and eternally satisfied and filled by God through a relationship with His Son Jesus Christ. God Himself created the void in your heart when He formed you in the innermost parts of your mother's womb so that you would seek Him. Alcohol, money, sex, drugs, power, influence, or fame cannot fill the emptiness in you.

We fell slaves to sin's desires in the Garden of Eden, but the cross of Calvary paid the penalty for those sins for all eternity. Our relationship with God was restored when Christ died on the cross. I know so many people who are doing so many good things to help people in an effort to win God's love and forgiveness. They believe that if they do more good works than bad works, God will let them into heaven. Theirs is a performance-based faith that is an abomination to God. When Christ died on Calvary He shouted, "It is finished!" The price He paid was sufficient to atone for all the sins of mankind forever. There is nothing more we can do to atone for our sins. Prayerfully read Ephesians 2:4–9, printed below:

> "But God, being rich in mercy, because of His great love with which He loved us, even when we were dead in our transgressions, made us alive together with Christ (by grace you have been saved), and raised us up with Him, and seated us with Him in the heavenly places in Christ Jesus, so that in the ages to come He might show the surpassing riches of His grace in kindness toward us in Christ Jesus. For it is by grace that you have been saved through faith; and that not from yourselves, it is the gift of God; not as a result of works, so that no one can boast."

Many people believe that their ticket into heaven is based on their behavior, good works, how much money they gave to charity, or the number of times they attended church. But God doesn't make us perform for His love and forgiveness because He is rich in mercy and kindness. It is a gift that is freely given. Are you trying to perform to earn God's love and acceptance? You don't need to. He loves you just as you are.

God never leaves us the way He finds us. He is interested in developing godly character in us through loving correction and by revealing the truth of His Word to us. God wants to expose the lies we believe about Him and ourselves and replace them with His truth. Don't ever forget that Satan is the father of all lies, and much of what we believe about ourselves and God is from Satan.

I believe there are three false feelings that many people become enslaved to in one way or another. They are especially profound in people who are abused. They are fear of failure, fear of rejection, and shame. When the seeds of these three lies were sown into our minds, they eventually took root, and the end result was bondage and slavery to false beliefs that have affected all our decisions. The damage they did to their victims is incalculable.

Fear of Failure

People who struggle with fear of failure often cannot accept any criticism at all, even when it is offered constructively. Criticism is viewed as a personal attack on our sense of self-worth. When we fail, we often experience anxiety, depression, and anger. These emotions often manifest themselves as either withdrawal or aggression. We begin to blame others for our failure and we become rude or totally reject the person we think is responsible, or the person who has gained the advantage in the situation. Then we begin to nurse the resentment or anger we feel, refuse to communicate with anyone about it, or go on a verbal search-and-destroy mission, telling everyone how we got the shaft.

Any standard you impose on yourself to obtain a more positive self-image is in direct conflict with the truth of God's Word. God's complete and unconditional love for you is not based on your performance. When you understand how valuable you are to God in Christ, you can begin to relax and see yourself as God sees you—completely forgiven and eternally valued.

The fear of failure can be absolutely paralyzing to someone who is asked to get up and speak in public. The prospective speaker is terrified that if he or she stammers or stutters or forgets to say something, he will fail to gain the approval of the audience—so he never gets up at all. Once we are freed from the fear of failure, we can soar to heights unknown to us before. You and I don't have to perform to gain God's approval. We see this in Psalm 103:1–12:

> "Bless the LORD, O my soul, and all that is within me, bless His holy name. Bless the LORD, O my soul, and forget none of His benefits; who pardons all your iniquities, who heals all your diseases; who redeems your life from the pit, who crowns you with lovingkindness and compassion; who satisfies your years with good things, so that your youth is renewed like the eagle. The LORD performs righteous deeds and judgments for all who are oppressed. He made known His ways to Moses, His acts to the sons of Israel. The LORD is compassionate and gracious, slow to anger and abounding in lovingkindness. He will not always strive with us, nor will He keep His anger forever. He has not dealt with us according to our sins, nor rewarded us according to our iniquities. For as high as the heavens are above the earth, so great is His lovingkindness toward those who fear [a reverential awe] Him. As far as the east is from the west, so far has He removed our transgressions from us."

Just think about what that psalm said. God pardons all our iniquities (sins), heals our diseases, redeems our life from the pit, crowns us with kindness and compassion, and renews our youth like an eagle. He performs righteous deeds for those who are abused, and removes our sins from His presence as far as the east is from the west. You see, God doesn't require you to perform to gain His love and forgiveness. Just come to Him as you are, failures and all.

Fear of Rejection

As a little boy I was overweight, short, and not very athletic. Whenever the neighborhood kids got together for a baseball or football game, I was usually the last one picked when sides were chosen. That process of selective elimination always cut very deeply into me and affected my sense of self-worth for many years. The message I was getting was that I didn't have much value and, "If we didn't have to choose you, we wouldn't choose you at all, because you don't have the qualities we want."

Rejection can be very painful, and the emotional damage from it can be enormous as it often negatively affects our responses to disappointment later in life.

Mary was a little overweight and had freckles. She was 13 years old when she entered high school. She had been a straight-A student all through grade school, but felt very self-conscious about her appearance. She came from a poor family, and her parents couldn't afford to buy her name-brand clothes. The kids in her class called her names and did not include her in many of their activities. Mary was deeply wounded by the rejection, and she began to wonder what was wrong with her. She felt worthless, alone, and so self-conscious that she didn't even want to go to school any more.

As time went on, Mary's grades began to drop, and by the end of the first year she was nearly failing. She was depressed, desperate for acceptance, and wanted so badly to be included by the in-crowd. Finally, in her sophomore year, she began drinking with some of the kids from school who were known as troublemakers. They accepted Mary—and they introduced her to drugs, alcohol, and sex. She soon learned that the alcohol and drugs made the pain go away for a while, so she began drinking more and more. The anger and disappointment she had bottled up inside her started coming out in the form of defiant and disruptive behavior in the classroom. Mary was finally expelled from school and later arrested for committing several crimes. By age 18, she had had two abortions, had been arrested several times, and had attempted suicide.

Mary believed the lie that "I am what others say I am," and it cost her dearly. Just think what a difference knowing the truth could have made in Mary's life if she had known and understood her worth in Jesus Christ. Fear of rejection is probably the number one reason that people are afraid to share their faith with others.

Fear of rejection can manifest itself in several different ways, including self-imposed isolation or by submitting to a controlling person in an effort to please them and be accepted. Oftentimes behavior can range from love at any price to loneliness at any price, shyness, passivity, or exaggerating the truth. Fear of rejection has kept millions of people from realizing their full God-given potential. Read and meditate upon the following verses:

> "Peace I leave with you; My peace I give to you; not as the world gives do I give to you. Do not let your heart be troubled, nor let it be fearful."
>
> —John 14:27

> "You whom I have taken from the ends of the earth, and called from its remotest parts, and said to you, 'You are My servant, I have chosen you and not rejected you. Do not fear, for I am with you; do not anxiously look about you, for I am your God. I will strengthen you, surely I will help you, surely I will uphold you with My righteous right hand.'"
>
> —Isaiah 41:9–10

We have a father in heaven who speaks peace to the storms in our lives and promises that He will never reject us when we come to Him. You and I are invited to approach His throne with confidence because of who we are in Christ.

> "Therefore let us draw near with confidence to the throne
> of grace, so that we may receive mercy and find grace to
> help in time of need."
>
> —Hebrews 4:16

Shame

Webster's Dictionary defines shame as "a painful emotion aroused by the recognition that one has failed to act, behave or think in accordance with the standards which one accepts as good; utter disgrace; to cause someone to feel shame by exposing his failures or misdeeds; to cause someone to feel inadequate by surpassing him."

Shame is a chronic sense of worthlessness that leads to the belief that, "I can't change. I am and always will be what I once was." Shame is often based on our inability to overcome past failures and a poor self-image of our own physical appearance. Many people see themselves as overweight, underweight, too tall, vertically challenged, balding, having a nose that's too big, disabled, bad teeth, etc., and they are ashamed of the way they look.

Are you angry with God for the way He designed you? Do you constantly compare yourself to others and feel unattractive? Do you constantly fall short of the world's standard of what is beautiful and desirable?

Others struggle with alcoholism, drug addiction, shoplifting, promiscuity, getting fired from one job after another, etc., and they feel powerless to break free from past struggles because they feel so ashamed. They have mentally reinforced the lie that, "I am what I am, and I can't change."

Jack grew up in a Christian home under the heavy-handed rule of his father, a pastor. Any minor infraction of household rules was treated with instant and severe discipline. Jack's dad ran the house like a military base where his decisions were never challenged by any-one, including his wife. When his father was around, everyone walked on eggshells for fear that he would go into another rage at any moment. No one outside of the immediate family knew Jack's father was so abu-sive. In fact, the congregation respected him as a real man of God. But when Jack was 16, the vice squad in a prostitution sting run by the police department caught his father. Since he was well known in the community as the pastor of a large congregation, it was published in the local newspaper. His father resigned from the church in disgrace, and his mom and dad divorced. Jack became the object of cruel jokes and teasing, and he was so ashamed of his father and himself that he dropped out of school. People pointed at him when he was out in public, and Jack knew they were talking about his family.

The only way Jack could cope with his shame was to withdraw from everyone he knew. He didn't want to be in situations in which he had to introduce himself to anyone. Making eye contact with people was almost impossible. Jack had been deeply wounded by his father's dictatorial tactics even before the incident with the vice squad, and it had colored his view of God as being angry and vengeful. Now he viewed God as vengeful, unloving, and untrustworthy.

Perhaps you have found yourself in a compromising situation that has caused you great embarrassment and shame, and you just can't seem to get beyond it and forgive yourself or the person who brought on the shame. Does it seem as though every time you're just about to put your past behind you, your mind recalls those old failures? Then does that sense of shame and worthlessness come back to haunt you? If that's happening to you, you must remember that Christ has thrown your sins into the sea of forgetfulness, never to be remembered. He isn't the one dragging up your old sins and failures—Satan is.

Satan is determined that you will never break free from your past, and he wants you to believe the lie that your worth is based on your performance or the opinions of other people. Has your life been para-lyzed by your fear of failing, your fear of being rejected, or shame? Jesus understands...

"The Spirit of the Lord GOD is upon me, because the LORD has anointed me to bring good news to the afflicted; He has sent me to bind up the brokenhearted, to proclaim liberty to captives and freedom to prisoners."

—Isaiah 61:1

You no longer have to live in captivity to your false beliefs. Christ came to set you free from the bondage you have lived in all these years. He is willing and able to bind up your broken heart and heal your wounds. God proclaims liberty for you through His Son, Jesus Christ.

If the abuse and rejection you have endured has left you struggling to trust God with your life, then read on. We will look at the unbelievable suffering Jesus endured during His ministry. If you still have a hard time believing that God unconditionally loves you and cares about every little part of your life, then in chapter nine you will see that He became personally acquainted with suffering and sorrow, greater than any human has ever known, because of His deep love for you and for me.

CHAPTER *6*

Cowards in the Kingdom: Case Histories of Domestic Violence

In my estimation, men who beat and abuse their wives and children are cowards and need to be firmly dealt with by the police and courts. Their behavior is absolutely inexcusable, and the consequences for their cowardly behavior should be substantial.

The following accounts of domestic violence are incidents that occurred in my jurisdiction and are ones that either have been investigated by me personally or are ones about which I have personal knowledge. I have chosen to include them in this book because they serve to educate those who have no understanding of the potential depravity of every man apart from God. They will also be a reminder to every woman who reads this book and is being abused that you are not alone. Every year millions of women are raped, beaten, and murdered by cowards in the kingdom. As you read, I hope you will especially notice the behavior patterns highlighted in each story.

The following incidents represent only a tiny fraction of the domestic violence that goes on every day around the nation. Many of the examples I could have chosen are so graphically violent and horrific that they were not included. All of the names of those involved have been changed to protect them.

Case 1

Many years ago, while working the night shift in the patrol division, I was dispatched to a home in our county because of a family disturbance. When I arrived I found the intoxicated husband sitting in a chair in the kitchen, waiting for the police to arrive. His wife, Sally, was standing in the living room crying and covered with black potting soil. **The drunken husband, Bill, had karate chopped the hearthstone and mantle off the fireplace and thrown them down the basement stairs. Bill had also karate chopped the baby's crib into pieces and hurled it downstairs, along with the mattress and box spring from their bed. He took all of the potted plants and dumped them onto the floor and onto his wife.** I arrested him and threw him in jail. Over the next few years I returned to this home many more times for family disturbances. I was unable to convince the wife to get out.

Then one night while I was talking to another officer parked in the turnaround of a major highway, a pickup truck came flying into the turnaround and slammed to a stop right in front of me, nearly striking my squad car. Sally jumped from the driver's side, ran between the squad cars, and yelled, "Help me, I want him arrested!"

I asked her what was going on and she said, "Look at me!" There was a full moon out that night, and as I looked up at her from a sitting position in my squad car, I could see that she was glistening in the moonlight. It looked like someone had thrown sequins in her hair and on her face. Sally said, "I'm all wet from him!" and pointed to Bill, who was slumped against the passenger side door, intoxicated and laughing. I asked Sally how she got wet and she said, **"He's been spitting on me for the last 45 minutes, all the way back from my parents'**

house where we went earlier today for a family reunion." A closer inspection revealed that she was drenched in spit. I immediately removed Bill from the truck and placed him in jail. Sally finally divorced him, and to this day Bill is still in trouble with the police.

Case 2

Thanksgiving is usually a time to relax, enjoy family and friends, and give thanks to God for all His blessings. But oftentimes the holidays can bring out the worst in people. Such was the case about ten years ago when a woman named Joan prepared a turkey dinner with all the trimmings for her husband, Robert, and some of her relatives. Robert didn't like Joan's relatives, and he **seethed in anger over the fact that Joan had invited them**. In an effort to relieve the discomfort of having to eat with his wife's family, Robert began drinking on Thanksgiving Day. By 3:00 P.M. the table was set and the turkey, along with everything that his wife had labored so hard to prepare, was placed on the table. Joan called everyone to come and eat.

When they walked into the kitchen, they were not prepared for what they were about to see. Robert was standing on a chair with his pants unzipped, **urinating on the turkey and all the fixings**. A fight broke out. Robert took the turkey and threw it through a window into the backyard. The police were called and the "other turkey" was taken to jail. Robert profusely thanked the officers for locking him up and told them it was the happiest day of his life because he didn't have to stay and look at his wife or her ugly relatives.

Case 3

In 1999 I was dispatched to a shooting involving a woman named Cheryl. When I arrived at the scene, I found Cheryl lying on the kitchen floor, bleeding from two gunshot wounds. Her ex-boyfriend, Tom, who was lying dead on the basement floor, had shot her. In the days that followed as I did my investigation, I learned that Cheryl had met Tom only six weeks earlier and agreed to move in with him. Cheryl knew very little about Tom but soon found out that he was insanely jealous. **Tom was constantly checking up on Cheryl, monitoring her phone calls, and frequently showing up at her place of employment. He never let her go anywhere alone. He sexually assaulted her on several occasions, and at one point he beat her up.**

After just six weeks, Cheryl couldn't take it anymore and decided to move out. The night before the move, Tom and Cheryl argued and cried all night long. Tom kept telling Cheryl he couldn't live without her or stand to see her with another man. One minute he would tell her to get out and the next minute he would beg her to stay. **Cheryl never called the police to ask for assistance while she moved out.**

The next day, at 11:00 A.M., Cheryl and a female coworker showed up at the duplex and started moving Cheryl's belongings into a rental truck while Tom was gone. While Cheryl was downstairs in the basement packing her belongings, her coworker was outside in the driveway loading the truck. It was then that Tom came back home, walked into the duplex, and locked the door so Cheryl's friend couldn't get inside. Tom immediately went downstairs, stood within three feet of Cheryl, and fired a handgun point blank at her head. The first shot miraculously missed her. Cheryl raised her right arm in a defensive gesture to cover her face, and the second bullet went through her wrist, missing her face. He fired a third shot. The bullet struck her in the right side of the jaw, traveled up to the area of the ear, and stopped. The impact knocked Cheryl backwards, and she hit her head on the concrete floor.

The impact from the fall knocked Cheryl unconscious. At this point Tom believed that he had killed Cheryl, so he put the gun to his own head and killed himself. A few seconds later Cheryl regained consciousness, crawled over the dead body of her ex-boyfriend, and made it upstairs where her coworker found her and called the police. Cheryl recovered from her wounds and went on to yet another abusive relationship, unable to break the pattern of dating abusive men.

Case 4

In the year 2000, a 21-year-old man named Randy was apprehended by our department on suspicion he had murdered his 16-year-old girlfriend, Carey. **Carey knew when she began dating Randy that he was extremely violent and awaiting trial for the sexual assault of a four-year-old girl. Carey also knew that Randy loved to fight and that he had been arrested for fighting with the police. She decided to date him anyway.**

During the interview, Randy told me that he flew into a rage after a night of drinking because Carey was bugging him and he was sick of her. Because she bugged him, Randy hit her over the head with a beer bottle and knocked her down on the floor of a building they had broken into. Then he took a large knife and slit her throat. While she was bleeding to death on the floor, he raped her. The rest of the details are too graphic to tell, but Randy had absolutely no remorse for killing Carey.

Case 5

A 21-year-old single mother, Francine, who had a child from a previous boyfriend, met an older man named Tony in a bar. **After just two months of meeting with Tony at the bar and knowing almost nothing about him**, she decided to let Tony move into her apartment. Within one month, Tony forced Francine to drive him to Oklahoma where they picked up three of his buddies. They came back and promptly moved into Fran's apartment. The girl was forced to work and support the four men who were now living in her apartment. They contributed nothing to the rent, nor did they buy any food.

Francine was constantly monitored by her boyfriend and not allowed to go to certain places or talk to certain people whom Tony did not know. She was repeatedly threatened, but chose not to call the police. She became a slave to the group. **Tony coerced Francine into going to a bank** and taking out a loan to buy him a new motorcycle because he had bad credit and no job.

One night Francine was overheard talking on the phone to someone unknown to this group. Tony became enraged and ordered one of the other men to choke her until she passed out. When she came to, Tony took a hammer and smashed both of her televisions and then beat her, fracturing her skull and perforating her eardrum.

Francine finally called the police, and I became involved. When I arrested Tony, Francine decided to run away to Oklahoma rather than to cooperate with the police. Eventually she was arrested on a witness warrant, and her assailant was sentenced to three years in state prison.

Case 6

Scott, a prominent homebuilder in our community, built an expensive home for an attractive woman, Carol, and her husband. During the construction of the home, Scott, who was married and had a family, began an intimate relationship with Carol. When Scott's wife found out, she went to Carol's house, where she confronted both Carol and her husband. Scott's wife was a decent wife and mother, but unfortunately her emotions got the best of her and a fight broke out. The police were called, and this mother of three was tragically placed in jail for domestic violence.

Both couples divorced, and Scott and Carol finally married each other, even though **Carol knew that Scott couldn't be trusted.** Shortly after the marriage, Carol learned that Scott was an **incredibly controlling person who played mind games with her, followed her, spied on her, and verbally abused her.** She finally filed for divorce, but Scott couldn't accept it and began **stalking her.** In spite of a restraining order, Scott continually broke into Carol's apartment and left roses, called her at all hours of the night, and continued stalking her. He was finally apprehended in the attic of her apartment by a K-9 police dog and was sent to jail for seven months. He became suicidal and nearly ended his life. He was released from jail, but he continued to violate the restraining order and was sent back to jail again. Today this once-prosperous family man has lost everything he owns, including his family, and is trying to get back on his feet.

Case 7

This case gives you an idea of the powerful influence a controlling man can have, even over a trained professional. Mindy was a psychologist, trained to deal with a variety of personality disorders. Several years ago she met and fell in love with Rick, a man who had been in trouble with the law. **Mindy knew Rick was a convicted felon, but she thought she could overlook his past indiscretions because she was not a judgmental person and felt everyone deserved a second chance.**

Rick had a **very dynamic personality and acted like a knight in shining armor.** He was handsome, sophisticated, and made Mindy feel like a queen. He would come and pick her up on his motorcycle and take her for long rides. He brought her flowers, took her to lunch, and had many romantic interludes with her. Rick told Mindy that he couldn't live without her, that he had never felt so in love with any human being in his entire life.

After only a few months of knowing Rick, Mindy let him move into her apartment with her. Almost immediately Rick began a barrage of verbal abuse and mind games that Mindy couldn't deal with. She began to notice that Rick constantly demeaned her professional accomplishments and demanded that she account to him for every minute of her day—he even questioned her as to who she was spending time with at work. He demanded that she give him money, never wanted her to talk to her family or friends, nor would he relay voice mail messages to her. Then Rick started to get very rough during sex, forcing himself on Mindy even if she were asleep. He would come in drunk and violent, throw Mindy on the floor, pull her hair out, slap her senseless, and threaten to kill her if she called the police.

Mindy finally became so terrified that she called the police, and Rick was arrested for domestic violence. Within one week **Rick had sweet-talked Mindy into letting him come back home. He cried, told Mindy that he would never treat her like that again, and begged**

her to take him back. Based on Rick's promises, Mindy allowed Rick back into her apartment even though a restraining order was in effect. Within two weeks Rick was battering her again. Once more the police were called and Rick was arrested, this time for bail jumping and domestic violence. Shortly after Rick was released from jail, he went back to Mindy's apartment and confined her there for three days while he beat her and sexually assaulted her. She finally got away and called the police. When I went to her apartment, Mindy showed me numerous holes in the plaster wall where Rick had run her headfirst right through the wall.

Mindy survived her injuries but was most distraught at how someone like Rick could fool her so easily in spite of all the years of training she had received to become a psychologist. Rick was sentenced to three years in prison and is now out on parole.

Don't ignore the warning signs of a battering personality. When properly applied, they are highly effective in helping you determine if the person you are having a relationship with is a batterer. If the women in the incidents I've described had known what to look for before they became involved, it would have saved them a great deal of pain and suffering.

One last word of advice. If possible, watch the way your partner's father treats or has treated his mother. If there is any sign of verbal abuse or physical violence, or if your partner has told you his father abused his mother, proceed with caution.

CHAPTER 7

Our Judicial System: What You Need to Know and Expect

Our system of law and order in this country isn't perfect. But based on personal experience, it's my belief that the vast majority of prosecutors and judges are competent, capable, caring people who dislike crime and criminals. Most prosecutors' offices are understaffed and underfunded, but despite these handicaps they do an outstanding job of getting criminals off the streets and out of our lives. Just look at how crowded our prisons and jails are. But that was not always the case with regard to the prosecution of domestic violence offenders.

In her book *Next Time She'll Be Dead: Battering and How to Stop It*, Ann Jones writes the following:

> Not until this century did a court rule that while a husband was still obligated to "teach the wife her duty and subjection," he could no longer claim "the privilege, ancient

though it may be, to beat her with a stick, to pull her hair, choke her, spit in her face or kick her about the floor, or to inflict upon her other like indignities."

Laws against assault were on the books in every state, but being intended to regulate the conduct of one man to another, they were almost never applied when a man assaulted his wife. Thus, many men continued to claim their ancient privilege, and law enforcement officers, uncertain of what the law required of them, and as one man to another—understandably reluctant to interfere in a fellow's "family" affairs—hesitated to look behind the traditional curtain of privacy.

In the 1970s, when women began fleeing to shelters, many of them told the same story. They'd called the cops. The cops insulted them, laughed at them, blamed them, put them down, or ignored them altogether. Some women had gone to court only to be told they had no business being there. Prosecutors and judges sent them home to "make up" with their husbands. Battered women's advocates and legal scholars set to work to make the laws better, stronger, fairer, and inclusive of women and to persuade the criminal justice system to come to the defense of women's rights. At last a thorough going paper reform took place, with many states adopting abuse prevention acts to strengthen the hand of the authorities and sharpen their focus on assault in the home.

Women worked with police, prosecutors, and judges—or tried to in an effort to help them see the issues from the women's point of view and to understand the seriousness of male violence against female partners. But battered women, still fleeing in growing numbers to shelters, reported little change.

Then some badly injured individual women and the families of some women murdered by husbands or boyfriends brought suit against police for failing to protect them as they would protect other crime victims, a violation of their civil rights. One woman, Tracey Thurman, won a suit against the police of Torrington, Connecticut, who had stood by and watched while her estranged husband stabbed and slashed and kicked her nearly to death. Awarding her substantial damages, a federal district court ruled that "a man is not allowed to physically abuse or endanger a woman merely because he is her husband. Concomitantly, a police officer may not knowingly refrain interference in such violence, and may not automatically decline to make an arrest simply because the assaulter and the victim are married to one another."

Over the years I have seen a number of domestic violence offenders who should have been arrested simply walk away from a family disturbance. The responding officer himself was going through a divorce and felt his wife was giving him a raw deal—he believed all women must be as bad as his wife. Or the officer had been divorced one or more times and resented making child support and alimony payments that he felt were too high. The officer's view of women in general was very negative and, as such, his sympathy was directed toward the abuser instead of the victim. Or the officer perceived the woman as a complainer, a whining nag who deserved what she got. I've heard officers say as they walked away from a family disturbance, "If I was married to that, I'd slap her up myself." The standard advice still given to many people in conflict is, "If you can't get along, just get a divorce and quit calling us."

Years ago I saw women arrested simply because they were crying hysterically or acted angrily when the police arrived and decided they were not going to arrest her abuser. When she began to protest loudly about the injustice being done to her, the abuser, smart like a fox, remained cool, calm, collected, and appeared to the officers on the scene as being the victim. Based primarily on behavior displayed in front of them, the officers began making comparisons between the two. They listened to the calm husband tell them that his wife was the cause of the problem, so, based on her emotional outbursts, they arrested her.

If you, as a victim of domestic violence, choose to call the police, I suggest that you do the following:

- If at all possible, try to regain your composure when the police arrive.
- If you need time to regain your composure, ask the officer for an opportunity to do so. But if you have been beaten and are injured, don't worry about regaining your composure. Your injuries will speak for themselves.
- Ask that you be given a chance to speak to the officers in an area where your spouse cannot hear you.
- Demand that the police and the hospital photograph your injuries for you, and then photograph them again several days later—that's usually when bruising shows up best.
- If for any reason the police decide not to arrest your abuser, ask them to wait a few moments while you pack essentials and leave with them. Don't stay if you don't feel safe.

The truth of the matter is that some police officers are on their third and fourth marriage or are living with their fourth or fifth girlfriend. They may be controlling, insensitive, or very dictatorial themselves. Even today some police officers respond to family disturbances and don't want to take the time, or are not given the time, to properly investigate domestic violence complaints. They simply announce to both parties involved, "If we have to come back a second time tonight, you're both going to jail." That statement may eventually cost a woman her life. Without caring, without realizing it, the officer has just given the green light to her abuser to continue beating her after they leave. The abuser knows his wife won't call the police again because she's afraid that she will be thrown in jail. The police have just told the woman that she has no credibility and if she bothers them again, she'll be arrested.

The other issue is this: police officers need to reduce the number of times they arrest both a husband and wife. Too often when the police arrive, both husband and wife are screaming or the woman is hysterical and difficult to interview. The officer is impatient and disgusted that he was dispatched to the call in the first place, and he doesn't want to take the time to wait until the people stop crying and calm down so he/she can determine the facts.

If you are fortunate enough to have a police officer with a stable marriage and family life respond to your cry for help, there's a high probability that he or she will be more inclined to assist you. Notwithstanding, there are also many fine single police officers who have never been married and hold a healthy view of women in general and will also make a good decision on your behalf.

Even though great progress has been made on behalf of women who have been victims of domestic violence, much more needs to be done. Because of the highly subjective and selective way some police officers made domestic violence arrests in the past, legislatures around the country had to enact mandatory arrest laws to force all police officers to do what was right.

Today, ignorance and indifference toward victims of domestic violence remain strong among a small minority of police administrators. Forcing older supervisors, police chiefs, and sheriffs to get with the program is not an easy task. In 2002, I witnessed this personally in the law enforcement agency I work for when I asked to attend domestic violence training at a daylong seminar—my request was denied. The training form I submitted to my division supervisor was returned to me with the words "request denied" written very boldly in red ink across the top of the form. When I asked why it was denied, the supervisor angrily replied, "It has absolutely no value to our department at all." I was stunned to hear his reaction because I was the only officer in a 140-officer police department who had any interest in investigating domestic violence complaints, and I had just worked an attempted murder/suicide that was directly related to domestic violence.

I was the only officer in the department who had a desire to acquire certification in the field of domestic violence training and a willingness to share it with my fellow officers. Training was critical to our department because the last time our agency had any domestic violence training was in 1983. Having been turned down by my supervisor, I went to the Chief Deputy and asked for training. His reply was, "We will not send you to any school that results in you coming back with certification as a trainer."

I finally flew to New York and went to school at my own expense to receive the training I was looking for. I returned to my agency and advised them of the civil liability that was hanging around their necks for failure to train. It was only after I mentioned I was writing a book on domestic violence and including a chapter on the backward attitudes of some police agencies that they finally relented and allowed me to train all 140 officers in the department.

A week after I finished doing the training, I got a phone call from a female officer beaming with pride because she had successfully investigated a domestic violence incident using the training I gave her regarding offensive and defensive wounds. She said, "A week ago I would have arrested both the husband and wife for fighting, but I knew from your training that the bite mark on the husband's bicep was there because he was standing behind her trying to strangle her and she bit him there in self-defense." Hearing that an innocent mom was spared from going to jail made it all worthwhile for me.

The Sheriff, Chief Deputy, and six department supervisors, including the one who denied my first request for training, boycotted all six training dates even though it was mandated by the state of Wisconsin. So you see, domestic violence is a priority for some individual officers and agencies, but others do just enough to get by. That attitude will change dramatically the first time the agency is sued for failure to train or the person in charge is removed from his position of public trust.

Police Liability

There are a number of ways that police departments and police officers can be held liable in domestic violence cases. The most common reasons are as follows:

- **Failure to take proper actions to protect a citizen.** This might include ignoring or minimizing the victim's pleas for help, refusing to provide safe passage out of the residence or area, etc.
- **Failure to properly enforce a court order protecting a victim.** This might include an officer willfully leaving the offender on the premises instead of ejecting or arresting him.
- **Failure to respond at all, or in a timely manner,** such as stopping to eat lunch or visiting with a friend instead of responding immediately.
- **Failure to provide information to a victim as provided by law.** This might include the location of a shelter or other community resources.
- **Arresting someone without probable cause.** This is most likely to happen in the case of a dual arrest where self-defense was not ruled out.
- **Exhibiting a pattern of treating domestic violence cases differently than other violations of law.**
- **Failure to adopt written policies governing the handling of domestic violence cases.**
- **Failure to train officers regularly.** Once every twenty years is not enough. It should be done annually and, in some cases, monthly during roll call.

Building a Case for Victimless Prosecution

Today in America a new trend is growing for officers to build a case against domestic violence offenders under the assumption that the victim will not cooperate or will recant her story while on the witness stand. It happens because victims are afraid, and justifiably so. Police officers can't protect anyone "all the time," and the victim may have to go back and contend with the abuser when the court case is over. Therefore, it's important for officers to understand that domestic violence victims do not have to cooperate with the police. It's wonderful when they do because it sure makes everything a lot easier. Police officers must learn to do more than just write a report or take a statement, though. They have to develop an evidence-based case that begins with reasonable suspicion, advances to probable cause, and ends in court with evidence that goes beyond a reasonable doubt— all without the testimony of the victim. I can guarantee every police officer in the country who does this that his/her District Attorney will deeply appreciate their efforts.

Some agencies treat the location of the incident like a crime scene, photographing any damage, collecting evidence such as blood, hair, or weapons, seizing letters, cards, or notes from the abuser saying he is sorry for past abuse, and retrieving a copy of the 911 call that was placed by the victim. These are a few of the tactics that will enable the District Attorney to successfully prosecute the abuser without assistance from the victim. If the victim cannot or will not cooperate, the police officer can still testify and present evidence. In an effort to stop or change violent behavior before it escalates into something far more serious, some police agencies and prosecutors are beginning to treat misdemeanor cases like they were felonies.

Let's examine the domestic abuse statute in the state of Wisconsin so you can understand how it's defined, along with some key terms and issues related to the enforcement of this statute.

1. Domestic Abuse [Wisconsin statute 968.075 (1)(a)]
Domestic abuse means any of the following engaged in by an adult person against his or her spouse or former spouse, against an adult with whom the person resides or formerly resided, or against an adult with whom the person has a child in common:

Intentional infliction of physical pain, physical injury, or illness
Intentional impairment of a physical condition
A violation of [s.940.225 (1) (2) (3)] (sexual assault).
A physical act which may cause the other person reasonably to fear imminent engagement in conduct [described under subd. 1., 2. or 3].

The two most important elements of the statute are:
The intentional infliction of injury
The fear of being injured

2. Mandatory Arrest for Domestic Abuse [Wisconsin statute 968.075(2)]

[Notwithstanding s.968.07 and except as provided in par. (b)], a law enforcement officer shall arrest and take a person into custody if:

The officer has reasonable grounds to believe that the person is committing or has committed domestic abuse and that the person's actions constitute the commission of a crime; and

Either or both of the following circumstances are present:
The officer has a reasonable basis for believing that continued domestic abuse against the alleged victim is likely.
There is evidence of physical injury to the victim.

If a police officer has reasonable grounds to believe someone is committing an act of domestic abuse, he/she must make an arrest whether or not there are physical signs of injury. Secondly, an officer shall arrest someone if they have reasonable grounds to believe that abuse will continue after they leave.

3. Primary Physical Aggressor

In determining who is the primary physical aggressor the officer should seek to protect victims of domestic violence. The relative degree of injury or fear inflicted on the persons involved and any history of domestic abuse between the persons, if that history can reasonably ascertained by the officer, may be used to make a determination. In other words, if the officers have been called to the residence in the past and know how verbally or physically explosive one spouse or the other can be, they can apply that knowledge to the present set of circumstances and make a determination as to who is most aggressive. The officers are permitted to make a judgment call as to who they think is most capable of inflicting injury or fear on the others present. That in itself may be sufficient for the officers to arrest one or both spouses if they believe that an act of domestic abuse has occurred.

4. Law Enforcement Policies [Wisconsin statute 968.075(3)]
Each law enforcement agency shall develop, adopt, and implement written policies regarding arrest procedures for domestic abuse incidents. The policies shall include, but not be limited to, the following: Statements emphasizing that:

In most circumstances [other than those under sub(2)], a law enforcement officer should arrest and take a person into custody if the officer has reasonable grounds to believe that the person is committing or has committed domestic abuse and that the person's actions constitute the commission of a crime.

When the officer has reasonable grounds to believe that spouses, former spouses, or other persons who reside together or formerly resided together are committing or have committed domestic abuse against each other, the officer does not have to arrest both persons, but should arrest the person the officer feels is the primary physical aggressor.

In determining who is the primary physical aggressor, an officer should consider the intent of this section to protect victims of domestic violence, the relative degree of injury or fear inflicted on the persons involved, and any history of domestic abuse between these persons, if that history can reasonably be ascertained by the officer.

A law enforcement officer's decision as to whether or not to arrest under this section may not be based on the consent of the victim to any subsequent prosecution or on the relationship of the persons involved in the incident.

A law enforcement officer's decision not to arrest under this section may not be based solely upon the absence of visible indications of injury or impairment.

The primary or predominant physical aggressor is not necessarily the person who strikes the first blow. In Wisconsin, the police are strongly encouraged to arrest the primary physical aggressor and may consider the following criteria in determining who the aggressor is: (1) who in the relationship poses the most danger to the other, (2) relative extent and severity of injuries, (3) size, strength, and bulk of the parties, (4) prior call history to that residence, (5) relative fear of each party to the other, (6) who is at most risk of future harm, (7) the intent of Wisconsin law to protect victims, (8) was the amount of force used appropriate and reasonable, (9) did one person act in self-defense, and (10) who is the most significant aggressor in this incident?

The legal concept of primary physical aggressor is another tool for law enforcement that allows officers to respond justly to a situation where the application of standard law would result in an unjust action.

The best way to help you understand this concept is by way of example. I know a man and woman who were married to one another for over 20 years. She was very petite, weighing about 95 pounds, a devoted wife, and a stay-at-home mom who had never been in trouble a day in her life. He was quite large at 6'1" and weighing about 220 pounds. For years the husband verbally and physically abused his wife. One night while they were at a wedding reception, the husband became jealous upon seeing his wife talking to another man and insisted that they leave immediately. Both had been drinking and were intoxicated.

During the ride home the husband began calling his wife some very vulgar names, and she suddenly exploded in rage and slapped him in the face while he was driving. He responded by backhanding her with his fist, breaking her nose and blackening her eye. As soon as they arrived home, the wife ran into the house and called 911. The police were dispatched. After interviewing husband and wife, they arrested them both on the grounds that they were both fighting. The officers ignored the intent of Wisconsin's domestic violence law, which is to protect victims of domestic violence; they failed to take the time to determine who the primary aggressor was, and they also arrested the wife because she admitted slapping her husband in the face.

The husband clearly met the criteria for primary aggressor. He was physically larger than she was, her injuries were much more severe than his, she was terrified of him, and there was great likelihood that he would harm her again. Officers need to look for the disproportionate response. If a woman throws a roll of paper towels at her husband and he responds by striking her in the head with a hammer, he is clearly the primary physical aggressor even though she may have started the disturbance.

The primary physical aggressor provision of the law allows an officer to recognize that one party may have instigated the incident but not arrest that person for his or her unwise behavior—instead, arrest the person who responded disproportionately to the provocation. This allows officers to act justly in an otherwise unjust situation and at the same time protect victims of domestic violence.

Police officers across the country are making too many dual arrests. Dual arrest should occur in only 3–5% of all disturbances, yet many police jurisdictions have dual arrest rates in excess of 50%. However, police officers cannot in good conscience just walk away from dual combatants because they will hurt or kill one another if left alone.

Still, too many innocent people are going to jail and their lives are forever changed by the trauma associated with a false arrest. In cases where the amount of force used was the same, the extent of the injuries is the same, and only after self-defense has been ruled out should a dual arrest be made. Prosecutors hate dual arrests because they are difficult to win in court. All the two combatants have to do to avoid conviction is invoke their individual right to remain silent by refusing to testify. Then the state has no one to put on the witness stand to testify against the other. Dual arrests should be made only as a last resort and only after determining that neither party had a legitimate claim to self-defense.

The negative consequences of a dual arrest are significant and long lasting. Let's examine just a few. (1) The victim will not call the police again. (2) The victim is not protected. (3) The victim may be denied public housing and child custody if convicted. (4) The dangerousness/lethality of the batterer increases. (5) The victim gets a criminal record. (6) The children are removed from the home and placed in custodial care. (7) The police department may face a lawsuit. (8) The victim is traumatized by the arrest.

Your Right of Self-Defense

Every person/woman has the right to self-defense. First let's look at two key legal terms and see how they are defined.

1. **Self-defense.** "The law of self-defense justifies an act done in the reasonable belief of immediate danger, and, if an injury was done by the defendant in justifiable self-defense, he can never be punished criminally or held liable for damages in a civil action." (*Blacks Law Dictionary 4th Edition*)

2. **Imminent.** "Near at hand, impending on the point of happening, threatening, menacing, perilous." Imminent harm means more than that the harm "may happen." (*Blacks Law Dictionary 4th Edition*)

Court Decisions

There have been numerous decisions handed down by courts all over the country as well as by our U.S. Supreme Court supporting a citizen's right to self-defense. Let's examine several key phrases contained in two court decisions handed down by the California Appeals Court in those self-defense cases.

People Vs. Arias (1989) 215 CalApp3d—"Self-defense requires both subjective belief and objective reasonableness."

People Vs. Clark (1982) CalApp371,377 (Cal Rptr 682)— "Justification does not depend upon the existence of actual danger, but rather depends upon appearances; it is sufficient that the circumstances be such that a reasonable person would be placed in fear for his safety and the defendant acted out of that fear."

There are several key elements to remember about self-defense:

- The person using force had a reasonable belief that she/he was at risk of bodily harm.
- The risk of harm was actual or imminent.
- The force used needs to be reasonable and proportionate to prevent or stop the infliction of bodily harm (i.e. the hammer used as a defense against paper towels is not reasonable).
- The duty to retreat does not include a duty to flee your home.
- Did the person (not necessarily the officer) believe she/he was at risk?
- Violence that is retaliatory is not self-defense.

In Wisconsin, our jury instructions for a claim of self-defense say the following: "A belief may be reasonable even though mistaken. In determining whether the defendant's beliefs were reasonable, the stand is what a person of ordinary intelligence and prudence would have believed in the defendant's position under the circumstances that existed at the time of the alleged offense. The reasonableness of the defendant's beliefs must be determined from the standpoint of the defendant at the time of the defendant's acts and not from the viewpoint of the jury now."

Let me show you by way of example what reasonable belief might look like. You are working in an all-night convenience store and a customer walks in with his hands in his pockets. He says, "This is a hold-up, give me your money or I'll shoot." At the time he announces his intention to shoot, he moves his hands in his coat pocket and leads you to believe that he has a handgun. You believe that he is going to shoot you, so you pull a gun out from behind the counter and shoot first, killing him. The police arrive and find that the robber wasn't armed at all. Do you have a legitimate right to self-defense? According to "People Vs. Arias" and "People Vs. Clark," you certainly do—if you have subjective belief and acted out of that belief with objective reasonableness.

If the robber had taken the cash, walked out the door, and started getting into his car to leave, and then you shot him in the back, that may no longer be self-defense but retaliation. The same would apply if your husband battered you and later you waited for him to go to sleep and then hit him in the head with an axe. That's retaliation, not self-defense.

My recommendation for any woman living with a batterer is to get out, but if you can't, buy a can of pepper spray and keep it in your pocket. It's highly effective on just about everyone and generally doesn't cause injury—but it sure is nasty.

Once you've sprayed your attacker, run like the daylights—get out of there, and don't go back. Keep in mind that if you leave pepper spray lying around in the open, your abuser can also use it on you. If you are sprayed, the only remedy is a profuse amount of water splashed on the face for about ten minutes.

The physical difference in size between the defender and her abuser can and must be considered by the police when they are determining whether or not to arrest someone claiming self-defense. For example, if a woman stands no chance of preventing someone who is physically stronger or larger than she is from inflicting bodily harm on her if she kicks him in the shins, it might be reasonable for her to use a weapon to prevent the harm.

Her weapon of choice might be considered the amount of force reasonably necessary to prevent the harm to herself, even if the risk of harm to her is not related to a weapon. Her weapon of choice might be a flower pot, a length of board, a lamp, or even a firearm. Cops do this frequently. Every time I have ever had to fight anyone bigger, stronger, younger, or older than myself, I used an amount of force greater than my opponent was using on me. If he were trying to resist arrest, I'd wrestle him to the ground. If he tried to punch me in the face, I pepper sprayed him so he couldn't see, or if he tried to hit me with an object, I struck him with a baton or threatened to shoot him. The way I reacted to his aggression was based on my reasonable belief that he was about to injure me. The burden I have, like all police officers have, is that I must be able to clearly articulate in writing why I used the amount of force that I did.

Would a domestic violence victim who believed that she was about to be struck or injured have the right to act in self-defense before the act took place? Yes!

When law enforcement, prosecutors, and the courts respond in a positive and supportive manner, the response has a very significant impact on both the victim and batterer. It sends a very clear message to the abuser that his behavior isn't going to be tolerated and that police consider his actions as criminal. The batterer often realizes for the first time that there is someone more powerful than himself who will hold him accountable for his bad behavior. Arresting the batterer provides safety for the victim, gets her into the criminal justice system, and sends her a message that she is supported. It allows the police an opportunity to inform her of the types of community resources available to her, such as emergency shelters and legal advocacy. The victim will remember the kindness and encouragement afforded by the police long after they leave. That type of behavior will eventually help her make the decision to leave her abuser.

Officers who are well trained and understand the dynamics of domestic violence don't engage in victim bashing. Saying things like, "How many times do we have to keep coming back here, lady, before you wise up and leave?" or "What did you do to set him off this time, lady?" or "If we have to come back here again tonight, you're both going to jail," are terribly destructive. When a victim of domestic violence hears the police make negative statements like these, I guarantee you she will never trust another police officer again. At a minimum, the police should be asking the abuser, "How many more times do we have to throw you in jail before you wise up and stop beating on this lady?"

But when a victim hears the police say things like, "When you're ready to leave, we're ready to help you," or "It's not your fault," or "You're not to blame for this," it will be tremendously encouraging to her. You should see how protective and compassionate police officers get toward domestic violence victims when the victim is their own mother, sister, or daughter.

One of the most important things a police officer should do when helping a domestic violence victim is to determine the lethality of the batterer. Just how dangerous is the batterer and how does a police officer make that determination? Here's a checklist that can and should be used by every officer:

- Have there been threats of homicide or suicide?
- Have there been fantasies of homicide or suicide?
- Does the batterer have weapons and is he likely to use them?
- Has the severity and frequency of recent violence escalated?
- Has there been a recent Order of Protection, divorce, or separation in the last six months?
- Is the batterer stalking the victim?
- Are children in the home or involved in the abuse?
- Has he ever talked in terms of owning the victim?
  "If I ever catch you with another man, I'll kill you both."
  "Death before divorce."
- Is he obsessed with the victim and family?
- Is he suffering from or being treated for depression?
- Does he have access to the victim and/or her family, or are they in hiding?
- Has the batterer attacked the victim in a public place?
- Has the batterer physically attacked the victim while she is pregnant?

After interviewing the victim, if an officer determines that the level of lethality is high, it is the officer's responsibility to advise the victim that she is in great danger and assist her to a place of safety before clearing the call. Many hostage situations are domestic violence related. When the hostage taker knows the victim, the chances of her being killed by him are very high.

When a victim is attacked in a public place such as a convenience store, bus stop, or place of employment, it should be viewed with the utmost alarm. This is an indication that the batterer has reached a point internally where he no longer cares who knows that he is a batterer. The restraints that once forced him to act out in private have now been cast off, indicating that he has reached a new level of desperation. He may be just one decision away from killing his victim.

Another major red flag to watch for is battering to a pregnant victim. When a batterer strikes a pregnant woman, he is telling her that she is so stupid and worthless that she can't even prevent pregnancy. The batterer now views her as physically disgusting and no longer desirable. Additionally, he may be enraged that he will soon be forced to financially support a child that he doesn't want for the next 20 years. This type of batterer is very dangerous.

Choking Versus Strangulation

There is a difference between choking and strangulation. Choking is an internal function of the airway that is blocked by an obstruction like food. Strangulation is a form of asphyxia caused by external pressure placed on the blood vessels and air passages of the neck. Police officers should use the correct terminology when writing reports. In my county, our prosecutor will give strong consideration to charging any abuser with "attempted murder" who strangles a victim into unconsciousness. If you have been strangled, seek medical attention immediately, as you could have life-threatening injuries and not know it. Tell the responding officers that you have been strangled and give specific details if you can remember them.

Offensive and Defensive Wounds

It's not uncommon for a batterer to say to the police, "Look at what she did to me," and then show them scratches or bite marks in an attempt to point the finger of blame at the victim. Police officers need to know that offensive and defensive injuries can be located on both offender and victim. Injuries are a road map to what really happened, and officers need to know how to evaluate those injuries.

When a victim tries to protect her face or the back of her head she will instinctively raise her hands and arms to fend off any blows or slashing. Consequently, it is common to see bruising, welts, cuts, etc., on the back of the forearms, along with swollen hands and broken fingers. Victims often turn, bend away, and present their buttock area to the attacker in an effort to protect their stomach, face, and head. The result is bruising to the lower back, buttocks, shoulders, etc. If the victim is lying on her back and trying to kick at her attacker, it would not be uncommon to see injuries to the calf area and shins. These are all classified as defensive injuries. Black eyes, cut lips, teeth knocked out, etc., would all be offensive injuries. It is possible for a victim to have both offensive and defensive injuries.

When a victim is forced to the floor and her arms are pinned down, sometimes her only means of defense is to raise her head off the floor and bite the abuser in the chest or arms. If she is being strangled from the front she will often rake the attacker's face with her fingernails or scratch the backside of his hands. If she is being strangled from behind, she may also rake the hands or bite the bicep or forearm of her attacker. When women are angry, they don't just run across a room and suddenly bite someone on the side of their hand or on the chest. These injuries are offensive injuries inflicted on the attacker by the victim. If the attacked has managed to strike the attacker with a weapon, he may also have defensive injuries that include swelling, bruising, broken bones, etc. Officers must take their time and demand to know from each person how they received their wounds. Wounds help to establish probable cause, primary aggressor, and ultimately who to arrest.

The Job of the Prosecutor

I spent a good deal of time preparing for trial when my testimony was required, and part of that time was spent in the prosecutor's office, going over testimony and evidence. I never cease to be amazed at the enormous volume of information a prosecutor must assimilate from witnesses, victims, experts, crime scene drawings, photographs, evidence that was seized, written statements, and police reports. Additionally, they are required to deal with hostile people who don't want to testify, emotionally charged victims and their families, as well as witnesses and victims who are frightened.

It's not uncommon to see dozens of pending case files piled up on a prosecutor's desk, chairs, shelves, and the floor. Many of them are buried under a mountain of paperwork. And after dealing with all of that, they still have to do battle with a defense attorney and convince a jury. Despite all of the difficulties associated with their occupation, most are doing a great job.

If you are the victim of domestic violence and your assailant has been arrested, you may be required to cooperate with the prosecutor's office and make several appearances in court to testify. For most victims who are already afraid, this can be a very unnerving experience. Courthouses and courtrooms can be intimidating if you have never been in one before. But don't forget that the prosecutor, police, and courts are there to serve you and protect you as best they can. If you find yourself required to make an appearance in court, call the District Attorney's office prior to your hearing date and tell him or his staff that you are afraid of coming to court. Most District Attorney's offices have a victim-witness coordinator who will stay with you while you are in court and will keep you updated on how your case is progressing.

I strongly suggest that you go down to the courthouse several days before your scheduled appearance and become familiar with the layout of the building. Find your courtroom, see where you are to park, and locate the restrooms. Spend an hour or so just looking around and getting used to the sights, smells, and sounds of this environment. You can usually walk into any courtroom and quietly sit down and watch while a trial is going on. The only courtrooms that you may be barred from entering are courts that are dealing with juveniles. If this is the case, there usually will be a sign on the door that says "Closed Hearing."

In important cases that I have investigated over the years, when I knew the victim or witnesses were afraid to testify, I usually had them meet me at the courthouse and I took them on a tour. A little familiarity seems to bring a level of calm and comfort and reduces anxiety. You are also welcome to bring a friend or family member with you for moral support. I do not recommend bringing small children to court unless they are required to testify.

In addition to what was discussed earlier in this chapter, there are a variety of legal terms and court proceedings that you should know about beforehand in order to understand and anticipate how the court system works. The laws, legal terms, court proceedings, and legal requirements in some states are similar to those in my state of Wisconsin since they are governed by our federal Constitution and existing case law. However, a number of states use grand juries to indict offenders.

Check with your local Family Violence Center, police, or prosecutors' office for information relating to the laws of your state. Most District Attorneys have people on their staff who serve as victim-witness coordinators to help you. Let's examine some of the legal terms and procedures that are common in many parts of the nation and used throughout the state of Wisconsin.

Miranda Rights
You have the right to remain silent; anything you say can and will be used against you in a court of law. You have the right to talk to a lawyer for advice before we ask you any questions and to have him/her with you during questioning. If you cannot afford a lawyer, one will be appointed for you before any questioning, if you wish. If you decide to answer questions now without a lawyer present, you will still have the right to stop answering at any time. You also have the right to stop answering at any time until you talk to a lawyer.

Restraining Orders: Harassment or Domestic Violence
Who can get one? You can obtain a domestic abuse restraining order if you are an adult who is related to, lives with, has lived with, or has

a child in common with someone who *physically abuses* you. The abuse may consist of, but is not confined to, kicking, punching, or striking by the other adult. The abuse can also be sexual. You can also obtain a domestic abuse restraining order if you are an adult who is related to, lives with, has lived with, or has a child in common with someone who *threatens* you with physical harm.

What does a domestic abuse restraining order do? A domestic abuse restraining order legally prohibits the abusive party from having any contact with you. That person cannot come to your home, your workplace, or any place temporarily occupied by you. If you wish, the order can also prohibit contact by phone, mail, or through a third party.

How do I obtain the restraining order? This is a two-step process. A legal advocate from your local family violence shelter or your personal attorney can also help.

Step 1: Obtaining the temporary restraining order. Obtain the required forms from your courthouse or family violence center and fill them out. Describe the actual abuse or threats of abuse. When completed, take the paperwork to the courthouse and have them read and signed by a clerk or a court commissioner. Then take the signed forms to the Sheriff's Department and have them served on the offender. If you cannot afford to pay for the cost of the restraining order or for the Sheriff's Department to serve them, the fee can and will be waived.

Step 2: The restraining order injunction hearing. Within seven days you will be required to attend a hearing in the courthouse to give some basic testimony, under oath, concerning the abuse. Your abuser may be there also and will be allowed to testify if he requests to do so. Keep in mind that, in addition, you can request that the officers who responded to your call for help be present to give testimony in support of you. If the court grants your request, the temporary restraining order will become an injunction that can last up to two years. During that time your abuser must surrender all of his firearms to the Sheriff's Department for safekeeping and will not be allowed to hunt with a firearm.

The harassment restraining order procedure is similar to the domestic violence restraining order procedure. The only difference is that this injunction legally prohibits someone from threatening to harm you, or from repeatedly committing acts which harass or serve no legitimate purpose, such as unwanted phone calls, coming to your place of employment, following you, etc.

Proof Beyond a Reasonable Doubt

Proof beyond a reasonable doubt is the standard of proof that must be considered by a jury in order to find a defendant guilty in a criminal matter. It does not mean "beyond *all* doubt," rather *reasonable* doubt.

Bond Types and Amounts

In almost every instance, a defendant is entitled to post bond. There are exceptions in very violent crimes, such as murder, when the defendant has a previous conviction for a similar crime. The type and amount of the bond is determined by a judge or court commissioner during an initial appearance to insure that the defendant will show up in court in the future. The judge considers the nature of the crime, how long the defendant has lived in the community, if he has a job, and if he has shown up in the past for other court appearances. If the crime is minor, the judge may allow the defendant to be released on nothing more than the defendant's signature. If the crime is more serious, he may order that the defendant post a cash bond of an amount he determines to be appropriate.

If the defendant does not have cash but has property (or a family member has property) that he is willing to sign over as surety, he may be allowed to do so. The judge will usually place additional restrictions on the defendant while he is released, such as no returning to his former residence, no contacting his spouse or girlfriend, or refraining from the use of drugs or alcohol. If the defendant violates the terms of his release, he can be arrested for bail jumping.

Bail and Bail Jumping

Bail is the monetary conditions of release.

Bail jumping is the violation of the terms of a defendant's release from custody while awaiting trial. The offender can be arrested and charged with a felony for violating this provision of the law.

Initial Appearance

An initial appearance is the defendant's first appearance before a judge or court commissioner after being arrested. The judge shall inform the accused of the nature of the charges by providing a copy of the complaint and informing the accused of the possible penalties for the offense set forth in the complaint. This is usually where bond is set.

Preliminary Hearing

A preliminary examination is a hearing before a court for determining if there is probable cause to believe a felony has been committed by the defendant. The preliminary examination shall be commenced within 20 days after the initial appearance of the defendant if the defendant has been released from custody, or within 10 days if the defendant is in custody and bail has been fixed in excess of $500. As a victim, you may be required to give brief or general testimony under oath concerning what your assailant did to you. This is not a trial but an examination of just enough information so that the court can determine if enough probable cause exists to bind your assailant over for trial. The defendant's bond may also be examined at this proceeding, and it may be ordered to remain in effect, be increased, or be decreased.

Battery [Wisconsin statute 940.19]

In Wisconsin there are three classes of battery. The first is simply **battery.** Whoever causes *bodily harm* to another by an act done with intent to cause bodily harm to that person or another without the consent of the person so harmed is guilty of a class A misdemeanor. This type of battery would be charged against an assailant if he were to slap or punch you, or throw you to the floor, causing bruising and swelling or minor bleeding.

The second type of battery is **substantial battery.** Whoever causes *substantial bodily harm* to another by an act done with intent to cause bodily harm to that person or another is guilty of a class E felony. *Substantial bodily harm* means bodily injury with a laceration that requires stitches, any fracture of a bone, a burn, a temporary loss of consciousness/sight/hearing, a concussion, or loss or fracture of a tooth.

The third type of battery is **aggravated battery.** Whoever causes *great bodily harm* to another by an act done with intent to cause either substantial bodily harm or great bodily harm to that person or another is guilty of a class C felony. *Great bodily harm* means bodily injury that creates a substantial risk of death, serious permanent disfigurement, a permanent or protracted loss or impairment of the function of any bodily member or organ, or other serious bodily injury.

Disorderly Conduct [Wisconsin statute 947.01]

Whoever, in a public or private place, engages in violent, abusive, indecent, profane, boisterous, unreasonably loud, or otherwise disorderly conduct under circumstances in which the conduct tends to cause or provoke a disturbance is guilty of a class B misdemeanor. This is the statute that is most often used when someone has been arrested in a domestic violence incident.

Harassment [Wisconsin statute 947.013]

Course of conduct is a pattern of conduct composed of a series of acts over a period of time, however short, evidencing a continuity of purpose [Under 947.013 (1m)].

Whoever, with intent to harass or intimidate another person, does any of the following is subject to a class B forfeiture: strikes, shoves, kicks, or otherwise subjects the person to physical contact or attempts or threatens to do the same, engages in a course of conduct or repeatedly commits acts which harass or intimidate the person and which serve no legitimate purpose. There are enhanced penalties in this statute that can be applied if the defendant has a previous conviction for this offense.

Stalking [Wisconsin statute 940.32(1)]

Course of conduct means repeatedly maintaining a visual or physical proximity to a person. *Repeatedly* means on two or more calendar days.

Discovery

Prior to trial, a defendant is entitled to discover (see) all of the facts, information, evidence, statements from witnesses and victims, etc., that the prosecutor intends to use against him/her at trial. Discovery enables the accused and his/her attorney to properly prepare a defense.

Motions Hearing

Motions can be filed by either the prosecution or the defense asking the court to make decisions on a variety of issues prior to trial. For example, a defense attorney might file a motion to have a statement by his client thrown out on the grounds that his client's rights were violated. A motion hearing may require your brief testimony but is usually confined to one or two aspects of the case.

Final Conference

In Wisconsin, a final conference takes place in court usually one or two days prior to trial. This is usually the last attempt by the District Attorney's office to get the defendant to plead out rather than to try the case. The prosecutor will make a final offer concerning punishment, and if the defendant accepts, the trial is cancelled and a date is set for sentencing. Keep in mind that judges aren't bound by sentencing agreements between prosecutors and defendants. Many times I have seen a judge impose longer prison sentences or larger fines than was agreed to by the parties involved.

Damage to Property [Wisconsin statute 943.01(1)]

Whoever intentionally causes damage to any physical property of another without the person's consent is guilty of a class A misdemeanor. Cutting the phone lines, tearing the phone off the wall, vandalizing the car, kicking down doors, breaking windows, and slashing car tires all constitute damage to property.

Probable Cause

Probable cause is "that quantum of evidence which would lead a reasonable police officer to believe that the defendant committed a crime." It is more than a hunch or suspicion, but less than the evidence required to convict at trial.

Surrender of Firearms

If your request for a domestic violence injunction is granted in the state of Wisconsin, the judge will order that your spouse/ assailant must surrender his/her firearms to the police agency that has jurisdiction in the community in which you live for a period of up to two years. Additionally, if you are convicted of domestic violence you must surrender your firearms under the Lautenburg Act.

Exigent Circumstances

The courts have defined *exigent circumstances* as:

* the immediate threat of escape
* the immediate threat of destruction of evidence
* the immediate threat of death or great bodily harm to the officer or the general public

If exigent circumstances do not exist, it is absolutely essential to have a warrant to enter the premises by someone authorized to give that consent.

If you call the police for help and upon arrival they hear a woman screaming from inside the house and they find that your door is locked, they will kick the door in, if necessary, in an effort to rescue you. The same applies if an elderly person calls 911 and says he/she fell down and can't get to the door. The police are permitted under exigent circumstances to force their way in.

False Imprisonment [Wisconsin statute 940.30]

Whoever intentionally confines or restrains another without the owner's consent and with knowledge that he or she has no lawful authority to do so is guilty of a class E felony. In other words, if you are caught in a domestic violence situation and your assailant ties you up, locks you in a closet, or prevents you from leaving, he may face an additional charge of false imprisonment.

Intimidation of Victims Felony [Wisconsin statute 940.45]

Whoever violates [s. 940.44] under any of the following circumstances is guilty of a class D felony:

* Where the act is accompanied by force or violence or attempted force or violence, upon the victim, spouse, child, parent, sibling, or grandchild of the victim or any person sharing a common domicile with the victim
* Where the act is accompanied by injury or damage to the real or personal property of any person [covered under sub (1)]

- Where the act is accompanied by any express or implied threat of force, violence, injury, or damage [described in sub (1) or (2)]

Sexual Assault [Wisconsin statute 940.225(1)]

In Wisconsin there are four degrees of sexual assault. Being married to your assailant is not a defense [under 940.225(6)]. In other words, your husband cannot sexually assault you and get away with it. You are not his property to abuse at will.

(1)(a) First Degree Sexual Assault

Whoever does any of the following is guilty of a class B felony:

(a) has sexual contact or sexual intercourse with another person without consent of that person and causes pregnancy or great bodily harm to that person

(b) has sexual contact or sexual intercourse with another person without consent of that person by use or threat of use of a dangerous weapon or any article used or fashioned in a manner to lead the victim reasonably to believe it to be a dangerous weapon

(c) is aided or abetted by one or more other persons and has sexual contact or sexual intercourse with another person without consent of that person by use or threat of force or violence

Second Degree Sexual Assault

Whoever does any of the following is guilty of a class BC felony:

(a) has sexual contact or sexual intercourse with another person without consent of that person by use or threat of force or violence

(b) has sexual contact or sexual intercourse with another person without consent of that person and causes injury, illness, disease, or impairment of a sexual or reproductive organ, or mental anguish requiring psychiatric care for the victim.

(c) has sexual contact or sexual intercourse with a person who suffers from a mental illness or deficiency which renders that person temporarily or permanently incapable of appraising the person's conduct, and the defendant knows of the condition

(d) has sexual contact or sexual intercourse with a person who the defendant knows is unconscious

(f) is aided or abetted by one or more other persons and has sexual contact or sexual intercourse with another person without the consent of that person.

Third Degree Sexual Assault

This statute covers a sexual assault in an inpatient facility such as a nursing home or mental health care facility.

[(3m)] Fourth Degree Sexual Assault

Except as provided [in sub(3)], whoever has sexual *contact* with a person without the consent of that person is guilty of a class A misdemeanor. This statute would cover sexual contact such as grabbing a women's breasts or feeling her behind even if she is clothed.

Sexual contact means any of the following:

(1) intentional touching by the complainant or defendant, either directly or through clothing by the use of any body part or object, of the complainant's or defendant's intimate parts if that intentional touching is either for the purpose of sexually degrading, or for the purpose of sexually arousing or gratifying the defendant, or if the touching contains the elements of actual or attempted battery [under s.940.19(1)]

(2) intentional penile ejaculation of ejaculate or intentional emission of urine or feces by the defendant upon any part of the body, clothed or unclothed, of the complainant if that ejaculation or emission is for the purpose of sexually degrading or sexually humiliating the complainant or for the purpose of sexually arousing or gratifying the defendant.

(c) "Sexual intercourse" includes the following [assigned under s.939.22(36)] as well as cunnilingus, fellatio, or anal intercourse between persons or any other intrusion, however slight, of any part of a person's body or of any object into the genital or anal opening either by the defendant or upon the defendant's instruction. The emission of semen is not required.

Federal Legislation

In 1994 the federal government passed the Violence Against Women Act, known as VAWA. This law provides that civil protection orders of state and tribal governments be accorded full faith and credit by the court of another state or Indian tribe and enforced as if it were the order of the enforcing state or tribe. If you obtained a restraining order against your spouse in New York and then moved to Wisconsin, and your spouse followed you to Wisconsin, the protection order from New York would be enforced by Wisconsin. If Wisconsin's time limit on protection orders was, say, two years, but New York's was four years, New York's time limit would be enforced.

The legislation also made it a federal crime for anyone to cross state lines with the intent of harassing, intimidating, or injuring that person's spouse or intimate partner, and as a result of such travel, intentionally commits a crime of violence and thereby causes bodily injury to such spouse or intimate partner. 18U.S.C. 2261(a)(1).

Now that you have a basic understanding of some of the laws that can be used to prosecute your assailant in a domestic violence incident, let's take an abbreviated look at what happens when the process begins.

If your assailant has been arrested and jailed and is unable to post bond, he will remain locked up in jail until trial. Jail is a good place for a man who beats and terrorizes a woman. This is where he himself begins to feel vulnerable and afraid. This is where the magnitude of the possible consequences start to sink in and he starts worrying about the future. If he tries to call you from jail, and he probably will call to tell you he's sorry, refuse to accept the charges, and hang up. In most jails, you can call the jail commander and ask that your telephone number be programmed out of the phone system so that you cannot be called anymore from the jail. Your assailant is entitled to a defense attorney, and if he is unable to pay for legal counsel, a public defender will be appointed for him at taxpayers' expense. The court officers will escort him from the jail to the courtroom and remain in the courtroom with him until the conclusion of the trial.

If your assailant's attorney contacts you prior to trial, or a private investigator hired by the defense attorney contacts you, my advice is to say nothing to them. They may bait you into a tape-recorded conversation. Do not answer their questions, and refer them to the District Attorney's office. If your assailant has been released on bond prior to the trial and is found guilty in court, he will be taken into custody by the court officers in the courtroom and taken to jail unless otherwise ordered by the judge.

Prior to going to court, sit down and write out on a legal pad what happened when you were assaulted. Pay attention to times, dates, threats, acts of physical violence that took place, and any background information leading up to the incident. If there were other witnesses who saw what happened, have them sit down with you and go over the details with them. Taking the time to do this will refresh your memory and make testifying much easier.

The judge who presides over the hearing is there to make sure that the process is fair and that certain standards of conduct are maintained in the courtroom. He's not going to let your assailant's attorney badger you on the witness stand, and neither will the prosecutor. All you need to do is tell the truth. If you can't remember something, just say, "I can't remember," or "I don't recall."

The prospect of having to go to court to testify against someone who may have beaten, raped, or terrorized you may be tough, but it is not impossible—you can do it. You need to prepare yourself by developing a new mind set.

Begin to understand and realize that even though you're going through a very difficult time, it won't last forever. A gracious God has spared your life. You're alive! You can learn from this tragedy and begin again, armed with newfound wisdom and purpose.

Psalm 34:17–18 says, "The righteous cry, and the LORD hears and delivers them out of their troubles. The LORD is near to the brokenhearted and saves those who are crushed in spirit."

God has not forsaken you. He loves you with an everlasting love, and He will protect and guide you as you walk through the process of assisting the criminal justice system in holding your assailant accountable. Walk into that courtroom with your head up. You are no longer a victim unless you choose to be. The bondage you were once forced to live under is now broken, and the healing can begin. You are physically free from his threats and physical violence, and you no longer need to live in fear.

God never intended for you to be a punching bag for anyone. You're a child of the King. Don't ever forget that God loved you so much that He sent His only Son into the world to die on a cross for you and me so that we might have eternal life. God is a God of fresh starts and new beginnings. Ask Him to begin healing your damaged emotions, your battered body, and your broken spirit. Ask Him to fill you with peace and hope before you enter that courtroom, and He will. He is faithful.

"For the LORD is good; His loving kindness is everlasting and His faithfulness to all generations."   —Psalm 100:5

CHAPTER 8

Escaping the Wrath of Your Abuser

You are not a punching bag for anyone—remember that! God does not want you beaten, abused, and misused by your spouse or anyone else. If you are living with an abuser, get out of that situation! God does not look favorably on any man who abuses his wife or any other woman. He spoke through the prophet Malachi concerning this issue and again through Peter about how women should be treated and looked upon. Let's take a look.

> "This is another thing you do: you cover the altar of the LORD with tears, with weeping and groaning, because He no longer regards the offering or accepts it with favor from your hand. Yet you say, 'For what reason?' Because the LORD has been a witness between you and the wife of your

youth, against whom you have dealt treacherously, though she is your companion and your wife by covenant."

—Malachi 2:13–14

"You husbands in the same way, live with your wives in an understanding way, as with someone weaker, since she is a woman; and show her honor as a fellow heir of the grace of life, so that your prayers will not be hindered."

—1 Peter 3:7

If your spouse has dealt treacherously with you, God has been a witness to it and will deal with him. God does not look favorably upon a man who abuses His daughters sexually, physically, or emotionally. If you are in an abusive relationship, have been threatened with violence, or have been assaulted physically or sexually by your husband or boyfriend, **get out now, but be very careful.**

Leaving your abuser may be the most dangerous step you will ever take. More women are severely injured or killed at this point than at any other time in an abusive relationship. There are a variety of reasons:

• They fail to plan properly.
• Many women underestimate their abuser's willingness or desire to physically harm them because he never got physical before.
• They fail to comprehend the danger they are in, believing that they can control their assailant's behavior through their own verbal threats and intimidation.
• They believe they can walk out anytime they want and, therefore, try to leave during the height of the conflict when the abuser is present and emotions have peaked.
• Some are caught by an unexpected act of violence when an enraged husband comes home, suspicious that his wife may be moving out on him.
• Others believe that if they wait it out, that everything will just blow over.

If you don't have the time to plan for your escape, get out even if it's only with the clothes on your back. You can always come back later with the police to retrieve your personal belongings. Your clothes and furniture can be replaced—your life cannot.

Never ever go back to your house or apartment alone after a domestic violence incident. My advice is not to go back even with a male or female friend unless you are positive your assailant has been arrested and is still in jail. This is usually the second deadliest mistake a woman can make. Countless women have returned to their domicile and have been taken hostage by their enraged abuser, who is now out of jail or who had fled the scene before the police arrived and subsequently returned to the home. Many hostage situations across the United States are directly related to domestic violence and result in murder/suicides. Remember the attempted murder/suicide I talked about in chapter seven involving Cheryl and her boyfriend Tom, who shot her in the face when she returned to pack her belongings.

Before I go any further, I think it's important to tell you that not all abusers will kill or physically injure their spouses. Most family disturbances never go beyond angry words and a few slammed doors as someone storms out of the house to cool off. Most family disagreements probably happen only a handful of times in an entire marriage, and are quietly forgotten or even laughed about later on.

My wife remembers a time when she was a teenager that her mom threw an entire plate of spaghetti across the kitchen at her dad, who had done something she didn't like. They look back on the incident now and laugh about it. Then there's the wife who flushed her husband's tropical fish down the toilet because she got mad at him, and the woman who dyed all her husband's underwear pink. On and on goes the list of strange, but non-violent, things we do to one another to get even.

I don't want you to assume that just because you and your spouse have had a heated argument that it's necessary to call the police, move out, file for divorce, or anything else. I don't want you to assume that because your spouse has raised his voice and used foul language that his behavior is necessarily going to deteriorate into a situation where you are in physical danger. Everyone is entitled to have a bad day now and then. We need to cut one another a certain amount of slack and expect that when we've verbally wounded one another, a time of forgiveness and restoration will follow. The safety plan is designed for those women who have an abusive partner who is about to cross the line from threats to action, or has already done so.

The Progression of Violence

If you are in an abusive home, if you want to leave, and if you have the luxury of a little time, formulate a written plan—but make sure you don't leave it lying around. If your abuser finds your plan, it may provoke him into a violent rage that could cost you dearly. I'll help you prepare your plan, but first let's take a look at when you should flee. Only you will know for sure when you have reached a point where your safety is in jeopardy. Consider the following "progression of violence" guidelines to help determine when the time is right. Keep in mind that these guidelines *do not* include an occasional verbal argument or disagreement when one or the other says something they later regret and which is out of character for them.

The guidelines begin at a point where there is significant anger, yelling, screaming, physical posturing, and threats that control you. The volume and frequency of his verbal outbursts are increasing. He is exhibiting behavior that makes you believe that he has gone from just being unhappy to a point where he is now threatening to make significant changes in the daily stability of your life and the children's lives. He no longer seems to care about your physical, mental, or emotional well-being, and he will settle only for having things his way.

Phase One: Verbal Threats and Intimidation
to Gain Control or Compliance

- "I'll divorce you and take everything."
- "You'll have nothing left to live on by the time my attorney gets done with you."

- "I'll take the kids while you're at work and flee the state, and you'll never see them again."
- "I'm sick of you refusing to do what you're told. Either do it my way or get out."
- "You can be replaced; there are lots of women out there who would love to have me."
- He prevents you from getting or keeping a job.
- He makes you ask for money, gives you an allowance, or takes your money.
- He refuses to let you know the condition of family finances.
- He puts you down, makes you feel stupid, humiliates you, or plays mind games.
- He controls what you do, who you see, and where you go.
- He uses jealousy to justify actions.
- He threatens to smash your family heirlooms, personal belongings, house, furniture, etc.

If your spouse has made statements or exhibited actions like these to you, I can almost assure you that on an emotional level he has made up his mind that he is going to file for divorce, has emotionally distanced himself, or will now begin to control you at any cost. Internally he is nursing a growing degree of anger, frustration, and dissatisfaction with you and the relationship. You are in immediate need of counseling and should seek pastoral intervention. Your husband needs anger management counseling. If he refuses to seek counseling, it would be safe to assume that his treatment of you will probably continue to deteriorate. His refusal to cooperate is a major red flag. Look out.

Most women who are hurting physically or emotionally will talk about what's hurting them with other women. They openly embrace one another, cry, touch, speak words of comfort, and talk and talk and talk until they get everything out of their system. Men are the exact opposite. When we are deeply upset about something, especially shame-based problems such as beating up a spouse, low self-esteem, insecurity, financial problems, loss of a promotion, etc., we withdraw into silent isolation. Out of fear of rejection, we refuse to let other men see who we really are. The result is often depression, anger, and bitterness. The more we nurse those feelings and negative thoughts, the worse the anger gets, and all it takes for an explosion is a few words from a spouse on the wrong day—then, look out.

Phase Two: Verbal Threats or Actions to Destroy or Injure— Psychological Terrorism

- "If you leave me, I'll kill you."
- "If you file for divorce, I'll kill myself."
- "I'll kill you and the kids before I let another man have you or them."
- "I'll burn the house down and blow up the business if you try to leave."
- "If you ever talk to me like that again, I'll knock you on your butt."
- "If you even talk to another man, I'll beat you senseless."
- He destroys property.
- He abuses pets.
- He displays weapons.
- He uses forced or rough sex against your will.
- He is the only one who makes decisions for you and the family.

If your spouse is making, or has made, comments like those above, or if his behavior is like that listed above, you are in extreme danger and must leave as soon as it is safe to do so. Your spouse is about to cross over a very important psychological barrier, and soon he will start getting physical with you.

If you have any pets, watch to see if your spouse has been abusing them. If you have seen him handling your pets very roughly or beating them, start moving fast. You're next. Or if your spouse has been unduly harsh with the children and is severely disciplining them for little or no reason, it's time to call the police and report him. If the children are being abused and you are aware of it and fail to act on their behalf to protect them, you could also be charged with being party to the crime of child abuse.

Phase Three: Physical Assault—
You must call 911 or flee immediately!
Behavior will include:
- Punching
- Slapping
- Hair pulling
- Kicking
- Throwing you to the ground, down the stairs, out a window, or out of a moving vehicle
- Beating you with any object he can get his hands on
- Stabbing, strangulation, or shooting
- Holding you against your will (false imprisonment)

If you waited until Phase Three before you fled or called the police, be glad that you're alive. Your abuser has crossed that psychological barrier I told you about in Phase Two, and he has made a conscious decision to give up control over his anger and emotions. There is no such thing as a person losing control. Your abuser has made a decision to give up control because he no longer cares about what's right or wrong—he only cares about having things his way and wants control again.

Once he has you under control, you will see him come back to you like a whipped puppy, cry, and tell you how much he loves you. That's hogwash. Your spouse doesn't love you; he loves controlling you. A man who loves his wife doesn't abuse her. Abusers belong in jail or prison.

Remember the following:
- There is a high probability your abuser will assault you again, and soon.
- Each assault will become more violent and more frequent.
- Each assault gets easier and easier for your abuser to carry out.
- You get physically and psychologically weaker with each assault.

I don't know whether or not you have ever seen a grown man or even a large teenage boy go into a rage. I have seen it many times in my career as a police officer. When it happens, it usually takes 5–7 large police officers to subdue that person without using deadly force. A person who is emotionally disturbed and goes into an unbridled rage is extremely dangerous and capable of anything. Their strength is multiplied many times over because of the adrenaline rush they are experiencing.

Some years ago I was with five other police officers at a family disturbance when the woman's live-in boyfriend went berserk. At 5'11" tall and 225 pounds, I was the smallest of the six officers. We fought with this man for almost five minutes and smashed up half the house trying to subdue him. We finally did, but not before one of my fellow officers was permanently disabled as a result of blowing out a disk in his back. The man we fought with was high on steroids and cocaine at the time.

An enraged man will pick up anything he can get his hands on and use it against you. He will grab an object such as a claw hammer, glass ashtray, baseball bat, hockey stick, kitchen chair, knife, or a gun, and have you dead before you hit the floor. Enraged men all over America have blown up buildings, shot police officers, killed their bosses and fellow employees, burned down their houses, and intentionally run over people with their cars or trucks. They have stalked their ex-wives or ex-girlfriends and ambushed them and their new friends. Just look at some of the high-profile cases in the last few years. An enraged spouse is capable of anything, and you must never assume that you can handle him; you cannot.

Finally, there is one more thing to consider if you are living with a violent person who has gone crazy. Don't ever give them a second crime scene. Here's what I mean: if you are faced with a life and death situation where you are in imminent danger of death or great bodily harm, and your abuser is ordering you to go with him to a more secluded area, ***don't go under any circumstances.*** Here's why.

He is probably either going to kill you, or rape you and then kill you. If you allow him to get you to a secluded area under threat of being shot or stabbed, when you arrive in that secluded area you will be totally helpless. You may be tied up, tortured, and then killed—with no one to hear your cries for help. What you must do is take your chances with your abuser while you are in a public place. If he shoots or stabs you, you may be able to summon help. A passerby is more likely to find you lying in a parking lot or a street than in a secluded area. If it's going to happen, make it happen in a public place. Never let your abuser get you in an isolated location.

Guidelines for Developing Your Own Action Plan: Surviving and Thriving

Plan everything on the basis of 12 months. Your goal is to safely **get out and get better** over the next year. Life may not be easy, but neither has it been up to this point, and at least you're alive. You may have to depend a lot on assistance from family, friends, church, women's shelters, and anyone else who can help you. At a minimum, you will need money, credit (if possible), transportation, employment, shelter, food, and emotional support. If you have children, you will need to provide them with education, medical care, clothes, etc. You need to start telling people around you that you have a problem—don't be shy about asking for help. Trust your circumstances to God and watch Him provide for you and protect you.

> "Indeed, the very hairs on your head are all numbered. Do not fear; you are more valuable than many sparrows."
> —Luke 12:7

> "But the Lord is faithful, and He will strengthen and protect you from the evil one."
> —2 Thessalonians 3:3

Leaving Your Residence—How and When

If you have to get out quickly with just the clothes on your back, get out any way you can—and run. This isn't the best way, but in an emergency it will have to do. Get to a phone as quickly as possible and get the police involved. If possible, stay in a public area until help arrives. Return to move out only with the police there with you.

If you have the luxury of waiting until a more opportune time, do it. Prepare, prepare, and prepare. It will make your life a lot safer and easier.

If you are certain your abuser is at work and going to stay there, or that he is out of town on business, make your move then. If there is any doubt about his return, call the police and ask them to stand by while you load up essentials.

Credit cards: how many do you have?_____

Whose name are they in? _____yours _____his _____both.
If they're in both names, your spouse may call and cancel the credit card once you have left, or he will examine your credit card bill when it arrives and see what town you were in when you made the charges. That may be enough information for him to start tracking you.

For debit cards tied to your checking account: can your abuser close that checking account and thereby deny you access to money? Open your own checking account in your own name—and don't let him know it.

Start a savings account in a bank different from the one where you normally do business. Have the monthly statement sent to your parent's home or some other address. Just before you plan to make your move, empty your joint savings account of everything. Don't leave him a dime. An abuser deserves nothing. If your abuser is your boyfriend, don't take anything that belongs to him or you'll end up getting arrested for theft.

Locate titles to your automobiles. Is the vehicle you are going to use for escape titled in his name only? If so, your abuser will report that you stole his car and have you arrested. Try to get the vehicle titled in your name. If all your vehicles are jointly titled, then there isn't a problem. Keep the title with you because you may have to sell the car, and without a title, it's impossible. Take the most valuable and most dependable vehicle if you can. Don't forget the auto insurance policy—you will need it in case of an accident.

Family heirlooms: things such as baby pictures, keepsakes, and other items of sentimental value should be rounded up and placed together so they can be packed quickly.

Grab your marriage certificate, the kids' birth certificates, school records, history of vaccinations, insurance policies, information relating to your 401k plan, social security number, driver's license, and every bit of cash you can get your hands on. If you need more cash, have a rummage sale or a garage sale and stash the cash.

Keep a supply of cardboard boxes somewhere nearby so you can pack the kids' clothes quickly. Make a checklist for yourself and each child regarding what basic essentials each one will need—things like inhalers, insulin, eyeglasses, prescriptions, etc.

Don't forward your mail to the address where you plan to stay. Forward it to a trusted family member or friend. Mail is easy to track.

Bring valuable papers like mortgage documents for your house, installment loan agreements, restraining orders, divorce decrees, immigration papers, or a green card. You need to be in control.

If you have pets, can you take them with you? If not, who can you entrust them to until you can get them? If you have livestock or horses, who will care for them while you're away?

Short-Term Shelter—1–5 Days with Family or Friends

• Where can I flee to in an emergency?

_____

• How long can I stay there? _____
• Does my abuser know that I might have gone there?
  ___ yes ___ no
• If my abuser knows I am there, is there anyone at that location who can protect me? ___ yes ___ no
• Do the people I am fleeing to know and understand my needs?
  ___ yes ___ no
• Is my safe haven really safe, or is there danger there also?
  ___ yes ___ no

If at all possible, get a cell phone and keep it charged and within reach. Keep important phone numbers with you at all times.

School

It doesn't do much good to make all kinds of elaborate plans to flee your abuser, move a few miles away, and then leave your kids in the same school they used to attend. When your abuser can't find you, the first two places he is going to look are (1) the school where your kids attend and (2) your workplace.

The kids need to be either taken out of school for a while, home schooled, or placed in a school unknown to your abuser. I can almost guarantee you that if you don't, there is a high probability your abuser will simply watch the kids get on the bus after school and follow them back to where you are hiding. Or he will simply lie in wait for you at the school and harm you there in front of the children.

Employment

Your abuser knows where you work, what shift you work, and what department you work in. Once again he will simply wait for you to come out of work and follow you back to wherever you are staying. Chances are that your abuser may even be friends with someone who works with you—and that person may be feeding him information about you.

If you do not have employment, try and take a job that requires you to work around a lot of other people in a relatively secure environment. I wouldn't recommend working the night shift at a gas station or a convenience store if there is any chance your abuser might accidentally stumble onto you. Working alone will make you very vulnerable.

If you must remain at your present job, let your supervisor know what's going on so that the company can take necessary precautions. If the company you work for has a security guard, also let him/her know in order to protect your car and be watchful for your abuser to show up. If they are informed, they can call the police.

Don't let your guard down just because nothing has happened in the last 30 days. Remember, in this day and age, people walk into schools and businesses and just start shooting.

If possible, carpool and change shifts.

Your Attorney

If possible, try to develop a relationship with an attorney you are comfortable with. You may need his services if the relationship ends in divorce. Be very careful. Some divorce attorneys are ready, willing, and able to financially abuse you in the process. Ask for references from the local women's shelter and from friends.

Your Church

If you are a member of a local church, I strongly suggest that you get in touch with your pastor immediately and tell him/her what your needs are. Oftentimes your church has ministries that reach out to women in trouble. Some churches maintain a food bank, a benevolent fund, and a second-hand thrift shop. The church may know of someone in the congregation who has an empty apartment you could use without charge, or someone who might loan you a car. Counseling services may also be available through the church along with employment training and resume writing.

My only caution to you here is that if your abuser knows where you attend church, more than likely he will show up also. If you have a legitimate fear that he will harm you, ask the church elders to remove him from the service if he shows up. He has no business being in the same church with you on Sunday morning. If he wants counseling, the pastors and elders can meet with him during the week if they feel there is any hope of reconciliation.

A Women's Shelter

Depending on the size of your city, this is probably one of your best options for the short term. You can find food, shelter, rest, and advice in a safe environment that is staffed by other women who have walked in your shoes. Many times they can plug you into an array of services that will be hard to avail yourself of if you are not staying there. Most shelters have advocates who can work with you and assist you in getting a restraining order or an attorney to help with legal problems. Many times healthcare can be accessed and transportation is made available. The shelter may also offer counseling for you and the children together as well as individually. Make sure you check out your local women's shelter. Many of them have done an outstanding job of caring for the abused.

Your journey will get rough from time to time as you transition out of your abusive environment, but don't give up hope. God is faithful and will make a way for you. The information I have just given you should help serve as a guideline for developing your own twelve-month survival plan. Break your plan down into categories like the example listed below. When you have the answers to these questions, and if you have the luxury of time, then consider making your move with the understanding that the next year could be challenging until you get back on your feet.

Preparing to Leave

What valuables or assets must I take with me?
Who knows I'm leaving?
How will I transport my belongings with me?

Leaving

Set a date to leave, if practical.
Who will be with me when I make my move?

___ police ___ family ___ pastor ___ friend

Is my departure permanent or temporary?

Shelter

Where will I stay?

How long can I stay there?

Is it safe there?

If I have to leave, do I have an alternate place to live?

Can my children be housed with me or will we be separated?

Food

How will I feed myself and the children?

How long can I depend on the charity of others?

Who can I count on at all times to make sure we don't go hungry?

Children

Where will they attend school?

How will they get there?

Who will pay for their medical and dental needs?

Employment

Who will hire me if I need to change jobs?

Who will care for the children if I have to work?

How will I get to work if I don't have a car?

Church

Where will I attend church?

Will the church help me financially or not?

Will my husband follow me to church if I go back to my old church? Will the church provide counseling and support? For how long?

If you have followed the guidelines from this chapter, you will be prepared to leave whenever necessary. Remember, you must be in control of your situation. Be sure of what you want to do—then do it.

CHAPTER *9*

Jesus, Victor
Over Violence

I was a professional law enforcement officer for 25 years, and I am grateful to Almighty God for allowing me the privilege and honor of pursuing this vocation. It was a challenging occupation that called on me to use the skills God gave me to serve Him and my fellow man. Being a police officer exposed me to some unbelievably good and unbelievably evil people and placed me into situations that few people outside of law enforcement ever experience.

I've learned over the years that sometimes we don't get the satisfaction of seeing the unjust get punished in this life. But I want you to know that the sovereign God of the universe will someday judge every single thought, word, and deed man has ever done on this earth. Not one single act will ever be forgotten or fail to go unpunished. You may be the victim of a crime and the person who has harmed you has escaped for now. But the day will come when a holy, righteous, and just God will deal with that person.

> "It is a terrifying thing to fall into the hands of the living God."
> —Hebrews 10:31

I worked the night shift as a uniform traffic officer from 7:00 P.M.–3:00 A.M. for the better part of 16 years before being promoted to Detective Sergeant. During that time I responded to dozens and dozens of fatal traffic accidents, mostly caused by drunk drivers. I've seen entire carloads of teenagers killed coming back from underage beer parties or a bar. I've seen people who had burned to death in fires. I've seen drug overdoses. I've seen suicides by shotgun blasts to the head. I've seen slashed wrists, hangings, asphyxiation, drownings, and murders. I've investigated gang violence, crimes against the elderly, and sensitive crimes committed against children by pedophiles. Recently I investigated the homicidal death of a 2-year-old girl who died as a result of being sexually assaulted by her babysitter. I was there in the emergency room when she died, I notified her parents, and I was present for the autopsy when the cause of death was discovered. I've interviewed women who were so badly beaten and abused that they were barely recognizable. Bar fights and fights at picnics and weddings were common calls. I investigated so many sexual assaults of women that I stopped keeping track.

I've been beaten up, thrown down flights of stairs, bitten, body-slammed in bar fights, attacked by women in the course of trying to arrest their abusive husbands, and urinated on. I've seen kids who have been beaten, abused, and neglected from the time they were born until the time the system sent them to prison for the crimes they committed.

About ten years ago, during a six-month period of time, I worked a fatal traffic accident in a small community in our county where five little girls, all 12 years of age, were killed instantly. They were standing on the sidewalk, talking together, when a car driven by a boy who had a history of seizures ran them over. The driver was traveling at a high rate of speed when he struck them and dragged them to their deaths under the car before he crashed the car into a large tree, seriously injuring himself and his sister, who was in the car with him.

During that same time frame I cut down from a tree a young man who had hung himself, and worked a fatal car accident that killed a college professor near Thanksgiving. One week before Christmas I pulled out of a car a young mother who was involved in a fatal accident that left her mother and infant child alive. I did CPR in the back of the rescue squad for 30 minutes as we raced to the hospital—she died before we got there. This was in addition to all of the other calls that I was dispatched to in the course of an eight-hour shift and during a time when I was working two fulltime jobs.

I've made death notifications at all hours of the day and night. You never forget the experience of waking up someone from a sound sleep at 2:00 A.M. to tell them that a son, daughter, husband, or wife has just been killed. I can barely describe what that does to the police officer who has to make that announcement. As I drove to the house, I would begin to get physically ill, wondering how bad it was going to be this time. I would wonder if there would be someone else in the house so the person being told didn't have to go through this alone. Would the person faint, or would they attack us in their hysteria?

Most refused to believe the news when I told them, and I had to repeat myself several times. They screamed, they cried, some begged me to tell them it wasn't true. Many went into shock, and their lives were never the same. No matter how hard I tried to break the news slowly and gently, it made no difference.

I've given you a tiny glimpse of some of my career experiences for a specific reason: I want you to know that I know what it feels like to hurt and to see the effects of murder and mayhem. I know what terror looks and feels and smells and sounds and tastes like. I know what you may be going through right now or are still struggling with from years gone by. I am mindful that what I saw on a daily basis is minute when compared to all of the crime committed all over the earth every minute of every day.

I have often wondered how powerful God must be, to be able to look down upon the earth and witness all of the mayhem in His world and still be able to love us. It's hard to imagine that God loves you and me so much that He sent His only Son Jesus Christ to die for us. Think of it: Jesus left the unspeakable, incomprehensible glories of heaven, where He ruled and reigned over the universe with unquestionable power and might, and took on the form of a newborn baby. He left an environment of total peace, holiness, and order to come to an earth filled with mayhem and unsaved rebels and make Himself a living sacrifice to pay for our sins.

Before we begin looking at the sufferings of Jesus Christ I want you to look carefully at several passages of Scripture that partially describe the majesty of God and what heaven is like. Consider what Jesus gave up so that you and I could have eternal life with Him by accepting Him as Lord and Savior.

> "Immediately I was in the Spirit; and behold, a throne was standing in heaven, and One sitting on the throne. And He who was sitting was like a jasper stone and a sardius in appearance; and there was a rainbow around the throne, like an emerald in appearance. And around the throne were twenty-four thrones; and upon the thrones I saw twenty-four elders sitting, clothed in white garments, and golden crowns on their heads. Out from the throne come flashes of lightning and peals of thunder. And there were seven lamps of fire burning before the throne, which are the seven Spirits of God."
>
> —Revelation 4:2–5

Just try and imagine a throne with a rainbow over it, with thunder and lightning proceeding out from it, and the God of all glory, with the appearance of a jasper stone and sardius, seated on it. It is beyond human comprehension. The thought of it all is too much.

"And when the living creatures give glory and honor and thanks to Him who sits on the throne, to Him who lives forever and ever, the twenty-four elders will fall down before Him who sits on the throne, and will worship Him who lives forever and ever, and will cast their crowns before the throne, saying, 'Worthy are You, our Lord and our God, to receive glory and honor and power; for You created all things, and because of Your will they existed, and were created.'"

—Revelation 4:9-11

"Then I looked, and I heard the voice of many angels around the throne and the living creatures and the elders; and the number of them was myriads of myriads, and thousands of thousands, saying with a loud voice, 'Worthy is the Lamb that was slain to receive power and riches and wisdom and might and honor and glory and blessing.' And every created thing which is in heaven and on the earth and under the earth and on the sea, and all things in them, I heard saying, 'To Him who sits on the throne, and to the Lamb, be blessing and honor and glory and dominion forever and ever.'"

—Revelation 5:11–13

This is the Sovereign King of the universe who spoke and, with a word, created the heavens and the earth. He is the One who is worshipped forever by countless angelic beings. This is He who came into the world as a helpless, dependant baby, born in a feed trough in a barn filled with the stench of animal waste. Jesus knew before He left heaven what life would be like, that He would be rejected, despised, and murdered by the very people He loved most—but He did it anyway.

From the moment of His birth, Satan inspired men to kill Jesus. If God had not intervened on His behalf and sent an angel to warn Joseph, Jesus would have been killed almost immediately after His birth. The violence at Herod's command was ready and poised to strike.

"When Herod the king heard it, he was troubled, and all Jerusalem with him. Gathering together all the chief priests and scribes of the people, he inquired of them where the Messiah was to be born....Then Herod secretly called the magi and determined from them the exact time the star appeared. And he sent them to Bethlehem and said, 'Go and search carefully for the Child; and when you have found Him, report to me, so that I too may come and worship Him.'"

—Matthew 2:3–4, 7–8

"And having been warned by God in a dream not to return to Herod, the magi left for their own country by another way. Now when they had gone, behold, an angel of the Lord appeared to Joseph in a dream and said, 'Get up! Take the Child and His mother and flee to Egypt, and remain there until I tell you; for Herod is going to search for the Child to destroy Him.' So Joseph got up and took the Child and His mother while it was still night, and left for Egypt. He remained there until the death of Herod. This was to fulfill what had been spoken by the Lord through the prophet: 'Out of Egypt I called My Son.' Then when Herod saw that he had been tricked by the magi, he became very enraged, and sent and slew all the male children who were in Bethlehem and in all its vicinity, from two years old and under, according to the time which he had determined from the magi."

—Matthew 2:12–16

Imagine hatred so intense that Herod issued a royal decree to his soldiers to murder every male child under two years old in an effort to kill the baby Jesus. There was a price on His head before He could take His first step or say His first word.

That same murderous violence that was intended for the baby Jesus is still being carried out on the earth to this day. Satan wanted to kill the Son of God, and he wants to destroy God's creation to this very day.

At age 30 Jesus began His public ministry and, after being baptized, He went into the wilderness. After fasting for 40 days and 40 nights, Satan came to tempt Him. While He was alone with Satan himself, Jesus was tempted in every way as we are, but never once gave in to the temptations. He understands our sinful weaknesses, desires, and propensity for getting ourselves into messes caused by our own human frailty.

Because He experienced the daily struggles and hardships of life just as we do, He has compassion and pity on us when we cry to Him for help in our time of need. If you have been the victim of domestic violence, sexual assaults, or beatings, and have never come to terms with your pain from those terrible moments, now is the time.

Perhaps you're angry with God and can't bring yourself to trust Him because you feel He didn't come to your rescue when you needed Him the most. It's okay—God is big enough for you to tell Him these things. Jesus understands and sympathizes with you. He knows what it's like to be blindfolded and slugged in the face, falsely accused, rejected, hated, misunderstood, spit upon, mocked, stripped naked, publicly humiliated, and crucified. He knows what it's like to die all alone. No one came to rescue Jesus when He needed it most.

> "About the ninth hour Jesus cried out with a loud voice, saying, 'Eli, Eli, lama sabachthani?' that is, 'My God, My God, why have You forsaken Me?'"
> —Matthew 27:46

Jesus knows what loneliness, despair, and isolation are like. He knows what it's like to have all His disciples run away and even deny they knew Him when the going got tough. Tell Him how much you hurt.

Tell Him how much you need to feel His healing hand, His gentle touch, His loving heart. He will be the father to you that, perhaps, you never had. Grace and restoration flow from His magnificent throne. Claim it now. Jesus will never turn His back on you. He gained victory over violence by trusting His Father.

> "I will never desert you, nor will I ever forsake you."
> —Hebrews 13:5

> "For we do not have a high priest who cannot sympathize with our weaknesses, but One who has been tempted in all things as we are, yet without sin. Therefore let us draw near with confidence to the throne of grace, so that we may receive mercy and find grace to help in time of need."
> —Hebrews 4:15–16

Throughout the Gospels we learn about a number of times when the Jews plotted to kill Jesus, or to seize Him, but God did not allow it because Jesus' time had not yet come to die. There was still a price on His head, and He knew it. He was a wanted man. Jesus knew that He was headed for a horrible death. But despite that, Jesus still reached out to people and met their great needs.

Large crowds of people pressed in on Him from every side, trying to get close enough to see or hear Him, often surrounding Him. He healed the lepers, the blind, the lame, the demon-possessed. He raised the dead and put up with 12 disciples who really tried His patience. Jesus set the captives free, fed the hungry with fishes and loaves, and turned water into wine. He hung around with the poorest of the poor, prostitutes, tax collectors, the unloved, and the unknown. He constantly found ways to restore hurting people and never complained about the demands that were placed on Him. At times exhausted, He had to get away by Himself to pray and rest.

Jesus knows what it's like to be exhausted, overburdened, and misused by people. He, too, was spied upon, stalked, and abused by evil men who sought to create mayhem in His kingdom. Cast your cares at His feet and leave them there. Jesus wants to meet you at your point of greatest need. He will provide rest for your weary heart and mind.

> "Come to Me, all who are weary and heavy-laden, and I will give you rest. Take My yoke upon you and learn from Me, for I am gentle and humble in heart, and you will find rest for your souls. For my yoke is easy and My burden is light."
>
> —Matthew 11:28–30

Let's take a closer look at the crucifixion of Christ in order to understand the horror of it all. Stay with me; I know it's been a tough chapter and the crucifixion of Christ is painful to consider, but it's necessary to help you understand how much Jesus loves you and how concerned He is about your circumstances. Jesus is in the business of turning our scars into stars for His glory. He came to set the captives free. Perhaps you have been held captive to fear, unforgiveness, bitterness, anger, resentment, jealousy, hatred, sexual perversion, alcoholism, or drug addiction. Jesus Christ paid the price for you and me on Calvary—He set us free from whatever binds us, whatever controls us. He has a wonderful plan for your life, if you will surrender yourself to Him.

> "'For I know the plans I have for you,' declares the LORD, 'plans to prosper you and not to harm you, plans to give you hope and a future. Then you will call upon me and come and pray to me, and I will listen to you. You will seek me and find me when you seek me with all your heart. I will be found by you,' declares the LORD, 'and will bring you back from captivity.'"
>
> —Jeremiah 29:11 (NIV)

> "Surely our griefs He Himself bore, and our sorrows He carried; yet we ourselves esteemed Him stricken, smitten of God, and afflicted. But He was pierced through for our

transgressions, He was crushed for our iniquities; the chastening for our well-being fell upon Him, and by His scourging we are healed. All of us like sheep have gone astray, each of us has turned to his own way; but the LORD has caused the iniquity of us all to fall on Him."

—Isaiah 53:4–6

Jesus traveled to the Garden of Gethsemane to be alone with the Father. The moment that He knew would come had finally arrived.

"Then Jesus came with them to a place called Gethsemane, and said to His disciples, 'Sit here while I go over there and pray.' And He took with Him Peter and the two sons of Zebedee, and began to be grieved and distressed. Then He said to them, 'My soul is deeply grieved, to the point of death; remain here and keep watch with Me.' And He went a little beyond them, and fell on His face and prayed, saying, 'My Father, if it is possible, let this cup pass from Me; yet not as I will, but as You will.'"

—Matthew 26:36–39

This verse tells us that Jesus was so emotionally distressed at what He knew was about to happen to Him that He was grieved to the point of death. He was lying on His face in the dirt, in the darkness of the night, crying out to His Father, saying, "If it's possible, Father, don't ask Me to do this."

Jesus prayed aloud in great anguish, crying and weeping before His Father. He went to the Father three times and asked Him if there was any other way to redeem man and still fulfill His purpose here on earth. Was there any other way besides the cross, did He have to drink the cup of death—a cup that was about to be filled to overflowing with all the filth of this world, full of all of the abuse ever inflicted on you...full of all of the hurts that have left you battered and bruised, fearful and alone...full of all of the shame and disgrace and humiliation that was ever inflicted upon you.

Because of Jesus' holiness and sin-free life, He had never known the effects of sin and He didn't want to experience the effects of it now. Even though His flesh was weak, His Spirit was willing, so Jesus cried out to His Father and said, "Not My will but Thy will be done." Jesus was in such agony that He couldn't make it on His own, so an angel appeared and strengthened Him.

> "Now an angel from heaven appeared to Him, strengthening Him. And being in agony He was praying very fervently; and His sweat became like drops of blood, falling down upon the ground."
>
> —Luke 22:43–44

The emotional suffering of Jesus became so great that, instead of fainting, His blood pressure may have increased to deadly levels and He began to sweat blood. His blood mixed with sweat and fell to the ground. Jesus knew the unbelievable pain, suffering, and hell that He was going to be subjected to. He understands the hell and torment that you have endured and had to deal with in your life.

> "While He was still speaking, behold, Judas, one of the twelve, came up accompanied by a large crowd with swords and clubs, who came from the chief priests and elders of the people. Now he who was betraying Him gave them a sign, saying, 'Whomever I kiss, He is the one; seize Him.' Immediately Judas went to Jesus and said, 'Hail Rabbi!' and kissed Him. And Jesus said to him, 'Friend, do what you have come for.' Then they came and laid hands on Jesus and seized Him."
>
> —Matthew 26:47–50

Jesus was betrayed by a kiss from a man He loved. Jesus washed the feet of Judas, knowing that Judas would betray Him. Has a kiss, a broken promise, a lie, or a broken confidence betrayed you? Jesus knows how you feel.

> "Those who had seized Jesus led Him away to Caiaphas, the high priest, where the scribes and the elders were gathered together. But Peter was following Him at a distance as far as the courtyard of the high priest, and entered in, and sat down with the officers to see the outcome."
> —Matthew 26:57–58

Jesus had just spent three years with Peter in a very close, personal relationship. They walked together, ate together, prayed together, and lived together. Peter could have spoken up on Jesus' behalf, but he didn't. In fact, when pressed about whether or not he knew Jesus, Peter denied three times that he knew Him.

Have you ever been beaten, sexually assaulted, or abused as a child by your dad or a stepfather and desperately hoped your mom would step in on your behalf and rescue you—but she didn't? Maybe the abuse you have suffered has come from an alcoholic or drug-addicted husband or boyfriend. Did you call your dad or someone whom you thought loved you to rescue you, but they refused to intervene? Jesus knows exactly how you feel.

> "Then they spat in His face and beat Him with their fists; and others slapped Him, and said, 'Prophesy to us, You Christ; who is the one who hit You?'"
> —Matthew 26:67

They blindfolded Him, spit on Him, spun Him around, and slugged Him. They asked Him to tell them who hit Him. That night they made fun of the Son of God. Has anyone ever made fun of you while they beat and humiliated you? Jesus understands your pain.

"I gave My back to those who strike Me, and My cheeks to those who pluck out the beard; I did not cover My face from humiliation and spitting."

—Isaiah 50:6

They pulled out Jesus' beard. Imagine how painful it must have been to have His facial hair pulled out! Jesus could have stopped the abuse any time He wanted. He could have called in legions of angels to kill everyone on earth, but He didn't. He didn't stop it because He knew that many of you wouldn't be able to stop the violence that's been inflicted on you. Maybe you've had your hair pulled out. Jesus knows what it's like to be overpowered by people stronger than He was in His human flesh. He gave up control of His circumstances and surrendered them to His Father, in perfect obedience to Him.

After being beaten and abused all night long, this bloody, battered man—the Son of God, God in the flesh—was marched across town and brought to Pilate, the Roman governor. Pilate found out Jesus was a Galilean and sent Him to King Herod. Herod laughed at Jesus and said, "So You're a king? Get one of my robes and put it on Him!" Herod sent Jesus back to Pilate, who brought Him before the crowd that had assembled outside. It was a tradition at the Feast of the Passover to release one criminal. Pilate asked the crowd whom they wanted released—Barabbas, a famous thief and murderer, or Jesus? The crowd demanded the release of Barabbas. Pilate asked the crowd, "What shall I do with Jesus who is called Christ?" and the crowd yelled, "Crucify Him! Crucify Him!"

Pilate turned Jesus over to the Roman soldiers, who took Him downstairs. They pulled the robe off of Jesus that Herod mockingly had placed on Him—then the scourging began. Scourging usually was done with a piece of wood that had nine leather straps attached to it on one end. Woven into each leather strap, a few inches from the handle, was a piece of bone or metal. Then another piece of bone or metal was woven into the end of the strap.

I have often wondered what kind of a man could inflict this kind of trauma on another human being. What has to happen internally for a man to turn into a person like this? And then I remember some of the cold-blooded killers I have dealt with, and it's not hard to understand. If God doesn't occupy the throne room of your heart, Satan does—and he loves killing and death. You're either influenced by God for good, or by Satan for evil.

The soldiers threw the robe back over Him, made a crown of thorns, drove them into His skull, and mocked Him, saying, "Hail, King of the Jews!" They blindfolded Him, spun Him around, and began to slug Him in the face—He never knew where the next blow would come from. He was probably knocked to the floor and then picked back up, only to be smashed to the floor again. I believe that Jesus was already in terrible physical condition from the beating He had received from the night before.

When the soldiers finally got Jesus to Calvary, they laid the crosspiece on the ground and placed Jesus on His back with the crosspiece under His outstretched arms. The soldiers drove nails through His wrist joints at the point where the hand meets the wrist. This part of the hand is where all of the nerves and blood vessels are located. Injuries here are most painful and render the victim powerless to use his hands. If the nails were driven through the middle of the hands, the weight of the body would pull the nails right through the flesh. The Roman executioners had the process down to a science. They were masters at killing.

Now they lifted Him off the ground. One or two men stood on each side, lifting the cross piece so Jesus was literally hanging from the nails in His wrists. They took the beam and dropped it into its notch, and then He rested on that. From this point on the executioner worked quickly because the condemned was suspended by just two nails. His chest would have gone into pectoral paralysis so He couldn't breathe—His chest muscles would have all contorted.

Jesus couldn't even catch His breath. He who is the "breath of life" could barely breathe. The soldiers jacked up His legs and laid one ankle on top of the other—His knees were in an upward position. They then drove a spike through both ankle bones. When done like this, the only way the condemned can breath is to push himself upward and grab a breath before slumping down again.

No one came to rescue Jesus when He needed help the most. He cried out to the Father, and the Father turned His back on His only Son. Jesus, the holy, spotless, sinless Savior, had just taken on the sins of the world. He had the sum total of all the sin that would ever be committed by mankind poured out on Him. Jesus became the sacrificial lamb, slain for you and me. A truly innocent man was paying the price for my sins, your sins, and the sins of the whole world.

I know people who cried out to God for help, but He didn't answer their prayers in their time of need...He didn't come to their rescue. I also know of many times when God *has* come to the rescue. Jesus understands. You may be wondering why God didn't rescue you when you were being hurt so badly. Perhaps God has a greater plan or a greater deliverance for you. If God had delivered you then, His purpose for you may not have been fulfilled anymore than if He had rescued Jesus before He was scourged and crucified.

God watched in horror as He witnessed cruel, sinful men killing His only Son. He saw and heard the scourging, the humiliation, and the mockery. He could have called in one angel and destroyed the earth that day, but He didn't. God looked down through the pathway of time and saw our great spiritual need to be rescued from sin, and He made Jesus the provision for us. He loves you so much that He was willing to let His only dearly beloved Son be that sacrifice. He forsook His only Son so that you, who had been wounded by sin, might be healed. Jesus hung on the cross for you and me.

Jesus gave up His spirit and died that day. Three days later, by the power of His mighty hand, God brought Jesus out of that tomb and raised Him from the dead. God wants to do the same thing for you right now. He wants to raise you from a spiritual death and give you eternal life. Jesus wants to fill your heart and mind with peace, and He wants to heal your terrible wounds. He is the mender of broken hearts, broken homes, and broken marriages. He is the sunrise from on high. He is the God of fresh starts and new beginnings.

Believe in Jesus Now

It's no accident that you are reading this book. God has led you to this because He wants to have a personal, intimate relationship with you through His Son, Jesus Christ.

> "For God so loved the world, that He gave His only begotten Son, that whoever believes in Him shall not perish, but have eternal life. For God did not send the Son into the world to judge the world, but that the world might be saved through Him."
>
> —John 3:16–17

> "Jesus answered and said to him, 'Truly, truly, I say to you, unless one is born again he cannot see the kingdom of God.'"
>
> —John 3:3

I ask you to pray this prayer with me right now. If you're already saved, if you already have a personal relationship with Jesus Christ, take this opportunity to recommit your life to Christ. If you have never committed your life to Jesus and have never had a personal relationship with Him, and if you want forgiveness of sin and peace that only He can give, now is the time. Settle the matter for all eternity right now. Pray with me:

> *Jesus, I'm hurting and in need of a Savior. I've lived a life of sin and emptiness. I'm sorry for my sins. Forgive me and cleanse me from all unrighteousness. Come into my heart and be my Lord and Savior. I give You control of my life and circumstances. Guide me and protect me through these difficult days. I need You and want You. Amen.*

Dear friend, if you said that prayer and sincerely meant it, I want you to know that your salvation has just been eternally secured for you. You are now a child of the King, and you may approach His throne with confidence, asking God to supply your needs. Every sin you have ever committed or ever will commit was just forgiven and forgotten by God because of what Jesus did for you on Calvary.

CHAPTER 10

Triumph Over Tragedy

Before you begin to read this chapter on the physical and emotional pain of abuse, I want you to know that there is hope. Here are the stories of four women who sometimes felt almost overwhelmed and beaten down with rejection, loneliness, and failure, but who found victory in spite of it all. If I had interviewed 5000 women, my guess is that I could have probably used all 5000 stories—many would be much worse than these.

As you read the stories of these four brave women, remember this: Never lose heart...never give up...win!

Testimony One: This Is Roberta

"The fact that I survived is nothing short of a miracle. God, in His great mercy, looked down from heaven and spared my life. Surely His mighty

angels protected me since I could easily have died from the force of just the first blow."

My name is Roberta. I grew up in a home with an alcoholic father who was often verbally abusive, very controlling, and worked constantly. Seeing the aggressive tactics of a controlling man as a child led me to believe that this was the way most men behaved and was probably normal.

I married my husband Ken when I was 20 years old. When we began dating, I saw the way he behaved and I was concerned, but not to the point where I was willing to end the relationship. Ken acted like my dad in many ways. If I had known then what I know now about behavior traits and warning signs, I would have recognized all the red flags, and I would have ended the relationship immediately.

Ken was ten years older than me and had been in serious trouble with the law as a teenager. I was aware he had spent time in prison for armed robbery and auto theft and that he also struggled with a drug and alcohol problem at the same time. I also knew he hadn't finished high school. But Ken told me he had accepted Christ as his Lord and Savior just before we met and that he was no longer engaged in his old sinful and criminal lifestyle. I was a new Christian, and thought I should overlook his past indiscretions now that Ken was walking with God and was part of a Bible study.

I noticed that in spite of the fact that he professed to be a Christian, Ken often used some pretty coarse language and was physically aggressive toward anyone who got in his way on more than one occasion. At one point I was concerned enough about his behavior that I gave serious consideration to not marrying him, but I couldn't bring my concerns to my parents—so I finally said yes to him.

Shortly after we got married, Ken became more and more controlling. He started breaking objects in the house during fits of anger, and at one point he put a hole in a door. Many times the damage was done when I was away from home. Over the next several years we had two children, and our marriage just kind of moved along, stagnating on "cruise control." By 1994 our relationship was deteriorating, so a group of men invited Ken to go with them to a Promise Keepers conference. The conference didn't make much of an impact on him, and we continued to put significant distance between us.

By 1995 Ken became increasingly more aggressive toward me, and he made verbal threats to kill me or shoot me with a gun, and one time he even told me he was going to shove a broomstick down my throat. He had destroyed pictures and slammed the toilet seat so hard that he broke it. Then one night, without warning or provocation, Ken walked up to me, put both his hands around my throat, and squeezed very tightly so I couldn't breathe. In one quick movement he picked me up off the floor, spun me around, and dropped me on the floor.

That incident was a turning point for me, and for the first time in our marriage I believed he was capable of hurting me. I went in to see the pastor of the Baptist church where we attended and told him what was going on. To my surprise and dismay, the pastor didn't believe me. He refused to confront Ken about his behavior and told me that I must be doing something wrong to cause Ken to treat me like this. Despite my objections, the pastor referred Ken and me to an outside counselor for joint counseling. From the moment we walked into that counselor's office, I felt it was not going to be a good situation—and I was right. The counselor immediately sided with Ken, so I never went back. I was extremely uncomfortable being counseled together because I was afraid to say anything negative about Ken since he was sitting right there.

I finally couldn't take the abuse any longer, so I filed for divorce. I remained in our house for three or four weeks after filing the papers, and then because of safety concerns I moved into a women's shelter with our two girls. The people at the women's shelter were absolutely wonderful to us. I will be forever in their debt for the kindness and care they provided. Ken was absolutely furious that I filed for divorce. He moved out of our home and made many threats to kill me as well as the female counselor I was seeing. My pastor knew I was living in a women's shelter, but he never once came to see us or offered any help from the church.

Then my hell on earth began. One night I left the shelter at about 9:00 P.M. and drove by myself to pick up some items from my home. I didn't think Ken was living in the house, so I thought I'd be safe going back there. I raised the electric garage door, saw that Ken's vehicle was gone, and assumed that the house was empty. I went inside and moved about on all three floors, finally making a phone call to a friend. While talking on the phone, I saw Ken's checkbook register lying on the table. It showed that he had just purchased a handgun from a local sporting goods store.

Before I ended the conversation with my friend, I mentioned my concern about Ken having a gun. What I didn't know was that Ken was hiding in the house, listening to my entire conversation. (I learned later that he had parked his car around the corner out of view and that he had been hiding inside the house.)

As I hung up the phone and turned around, I saw my husband coming at me, armed with a large wooden knurl post that was used to anchor the banister railing in the staircase. He had the post raised over his head with both hands, and I could see the rage in his eyes as he came at me. I screamed and put my hands up to protect myself. Then he hit me.

I remember him hitting me in the head so hard that I thought my head would explode. I can't remember whether or not he said anything to me after that, but he sounded like he was growling. The next thing I can recall is being in the garage near the step by the entrance door to the house. My head was spinning and I was fighting to remain conscious. I remember lying on the cold concrete garage floor while Ken clubbed me in the arms and head again and again. I remember being beaten while I tried to get up. I don't remember anything else.

The police report indicates that I was beaten in several locations in the house and garage. It shows that there was a trail of blood 92 feet long, and that the blood spatters indicated that I was struck in the head while I was lying prostrate on the garage floor.

For reasons only God will probably ever know, Ken stopped beating me, loaded me into his car, and took me to the emergency room of one of our area hospitals 15 miles away. According to the police report, he dropped me off in the parking lot, left, and then returned armed with the 38-caliber revolver that he had purchased from a sporting goods store. By this time the police had been called by hospital security, and they responded in time to apprehend Ken before he got inside the hospital. It was later determined that Ken had returned with the intention of killing himself. At the time of his arrest, he was covered in my blood. An examination of Ken's car revealed that my blood was all over the inside and outside of it, even on the ceiling.

Photographs taken by law enforcement officers and the surgeon show that my skull was smashed like a puzzle. The blows I received were so forceful that part of my skullcap was blown off and my brain was exposed. I had massive bruises extending from my hands to my elbows. Bones in both hands were broken, one eye was black and blue and swollen shut, and I had severe lacerations to my face.

I spent two weeks recovering in intensive care and many weeks in intermediate care. The hospital staff was wonderful to me, and when I entered intermediate care, they allowed my kids to stay overnight and sleep with me in the same bed. The only bad part was that they saw the effects of the beating every time they came to the hospital. My head was shaved, and I looked like the living dead—it traumatized them very badly. I lost my ability to smell and taste for the rest of my life, but I didn't lose my speech or motor skills. I finally recovered to a point where I was released from the hospital, but I hated to leave because I felt safe there, and so did the kids. (Oh, by the way, my pastor—who didn't believe me when I told him Ken was abusing me, the one who insisted I must have done something wrong to make Ken upset—sent me a "get well" card in the mail after he read in the paper that my husband had been charged with attempted murder.)

We went back to the women's shelter and they took us in again. These wonderful people allowed my mom to come in and stay with us so she could change the bandages on my head and clean my wounds. I remember I couldn't wash my hair until the risk of infection subsided —several weeks. Six more months of therapy followed after I left the hospital before I was semi-functional again.

The fact that I survived is nothing short of a miracle. God, in His great mercy, looked down from heaven and spared my life. Surely His mighty angels protected me since I could easily have died from the force of just the first blow. Ken could have dumped my body out in the woods or a field and left me to die of exposure after he knocked me unconscious. Even worse, he could have used the gun he bought and carried out his earlier threats to shoot me in the head—I would have assuredly died from my injuries. I could have ended up blind, mute, or in a vegetative state, but none of those things happened. That's a miracle, and I give God all the credit for His providential care. I learned that once the story became public, people from all over the country began praying for me. God continued to meet my every need.

One of the reasons the girls and I had to go back to the women's shelter was because the judge set bail low enough that my husband was released from custody for six months before the trial. I couldn't believe that a judge would let him out, but he did. I was terrified to go anywhere for fear Ken would find the kids and me and kill us. The girls were suffering from posttraumatic stress, were depressed, and had panic attacks. What was even more outrageous was that our pastor invited my husband to come back and attend church there while he was out on bail. At one point I ran into a woman who used to be in our Bible study. My head was still shaved with just a tiny bit of hair stubble sticking out, and many of my scars were visible even though I wore a stocking cap. The woman had the audacity to stop me and tell me that she had just seen my husband at their Bible study.

A trial was held and my husband was convicted of attempted murder. Even after he was found guilty, the judge allowed him to remain free for 30 more days to give him time to get his affairs in order. The girls and I continued to live in fear for another month until the sentencing. Finally my husband was sentenced and received 30 years in prison. Ken has tried to find out where I'm living and has taken me back to court over several issues. What amazes me is that he still cites Scripture in his correspondence. He has never admitted his guilt or said he was sorry.

Nevertheless, God is still faithful and continues to provide for me. The girls and I struggle with a number of issues relating to the abuse that only time and God's amazing grace will heal. If my testimony saves the life of just one woman, then my pain and suffering will not have been in vain.

Testimony Two: Susan's Story

"I finally ran away at age 17, when I couldn't endure the abuse anymore. The police caught me and took me home. I had never reported the abuse because calling the police would have meant death for me, so when I was caught I was returned to my father. He was furious that I had left."

I grew up in a home believing that my stepmother really was my mom. It wasn't until I was in my early teens that I discovered that my biological mother lived elsewhere. My father had told me that he came home from World War II when I was 14 months old and that he had found me in a crib in a filthy apartment overflowing with garbage and maggots. He said I was covered in my own excrement and, because of these conditions, he felt it necessary to take me and move away from my mother. I found out later that all of that was a lie.

My father was an upstanding Mormon. I have clear recollections of his verbal abuse toward me as a child and of the extent he went to to let me know that no matter what I did, it would never be good enough. If I came home with a B average on my report card, he would tell me, "That isn't good enough. Get all As." By the age of ten, the physical abuse had started. My father was a very big man, weighing about 250 pounds. At the dinner table, he would force me to eat twice as much food as he did in the same amount of time. If I didn't, he would take whatever I hadn't consumed and put it in the refrigerator for the next meal—then I would be forced to eat that plus the next meal. I can remember forcing myself to throw up just so I could get all the food in.

I spent nearly six years confined to my bedroom. I was allowed out only to go to school and eat meals. I spent a lot of time isolated and alone. I recall times when my father pointed a loaded gun at me, cocked the hammer back, and threatened to shoot me. On one occasion he wrapped an electrical cord around my neck and choked me. Once he took me out in the desert, beat me with a board, and told me, "Go ahead and scream; nobody can hear you out here."

I was absolutely terrified of this man because I knew he was willing and capable of killing me. I don't know why he didn't love me other than he may have seen my mother in me. I believe he hated her so much that this was his way of getting back at her. Until the age of 17, I was routinely forced to take down my pants, lie face down on the bed, and grab hold of either side of it while he spanked me on my bare bottom. This was a shameful and embarrassing thing for me to endure, but to protest would have been even worse.

One time I was struck with a baseball bat and nearly passed out from the beating. If my father walked past my bedroom while I was exiting the room, he would grab my long hair, wrap his fist in it, and throw me to the floor. I finally cut my hair, and I wear it short even today so no one can grab it. My scalp became so sensitive because of the pulling of my hair that even my babies couldn't touch it when they were little.

At age 16 I finally located my biological mother and, with the consent of my father, I spent a week with her. I never did find out why he let me visit her, but I found her to be a decent person who was very kind to me. At the end of a week I had to return home, but 38 years later I would find her again and learn about all the lies my father had told me.

I finally ran away at age 17, when I couldn't endure the abuse anymore. The police caught me and took me home. I had never reported the abuse because calling the police would have meant death for me, so when I was caught I was returned to my father. He was furious that I had left.

I became a master at hiding my injuries with clothes and makeup, and I never told anyone about what I was enduring at home. I was not allowed to get involved in any extra-curricular activities at school, such as a dance, basketball, track, or music. In four years, I never once attended an after-school function. There was a time that I missed almost a month of school recovering from injuries I sustained from his beatings. My father constantly struck me on the side of the head with his open hand, causing injuries to my ear and hearing.

My stepmother never stepped in and stopped the abuse, and she often wrote excuses to the school saying that I was sick for one reason or another. Eventually she, too, began to abuse me, and at one time she struck me in the head with a spiked high heel and dug her nails into my arm until it bled. In those days, things were much different than they are now, and even with all the signs of abuse, no one seemed to notice.

My father rarely ever met with his relatives. When he did, I was forced to sit on the floor at his feet and not move. I was rarely ever allowed to talk to my cousins and other family members because Dad was concerned I might tell someone what he was doing to me.

Several months after running away the first time, I ran away again. This time the police caught me and I was put in a juvenile facility and labeled as incorrigible. A short time later I turned 18 and was released on my own.

Shortly after I left the juvenile facility in 1963, I met and married my first husband. Severe physical abuse and a sexual assault marred the relationship. Without realizing it, I had married someone just like my father. One of the beatings I received took place in his parents' backyard—it was so bad that it resulted in a miscarriage.

Something snapped inside me the day I had the miscarriage. I decided then and there that I was never going to let another human being ever beat me again. I told my husband that day, "If you ever touch me again, I'll kill you. Sooner or later you will have to go to sleep and when you do, I'll cut your heart out." I divorced him and waited two years before marrying again.

I was still looking for someone to love and care for me. I just wanted someone to love me for being me. I wanted to find someone who wouldn't beat on me. This time I married a man with a drug and alcohol problem. We had two children, and it wasn't long before he started being verbally abusive toward me. This was soon followed by threats of physical violence, and finally the threats were carried out.

One night when I was seven months pregnant with our second child, I was fixing dinner. Our little boy came in the kitchen and said, "Mommy, I have to go to the bathroom." My husband walked in and told our son to sit on a chair and hold it. He also told him that if he wet his pants, he'd beat him. I told him to pick on somebody his own size, and when I said that, my husband grabbed me by the head and bent me backwards until my head was in the sink. I was able to get our son out of the apartment, but a few moments later my husband tried to throw me down a flight of stairs outside. If the neighborhood men who saw him trying to throw me down the stairs had not intervened, I would have been hurt very seriously once again. In 1973, shortly after the baby was born, I filed for my second divorce.

By now almost ten years had passed since I had seen my father, and I had an overwhelming desire to see him again. During those years I visited a number of different churches, searching for answers and trying to find a way to get rid of the anger and bitterness I had inside. None of them ever seemed quite right for me, so I kept searching.

Finally, when my last baby was born, my father and stepmother came to visit me. I watched in stunned disbelief as that little old grayhaired man struggled to climb up the steps to my apartment. His once powerful 250-pound frame was now reduced to childlike proportions. He looked so pitiful and helpless.

The effects of anger and time had bent him over and had taken a terrible toll on my dad. Even though I wasn't a Christian yet, that was the day I found the strength to forgive him. About a year later I went to visit him at his home, and while I was in the kitchen, he walked up next to me and mockingly threw a punch to my shoulder and said, "Good morning." I did the same thing back to him, but he reeled backwards, believing I was going to deck him. In that moment I saw years of abuse recalled in his facial expression, and I knew then that I was capable of loving him again.

My dad died unexpectedly a short time later. It was only then that I realized how much I really loved him in spite of the terrible abuse he had inflicted on me. When I received the news of his death, I was so hurt I thought my heart would explode. My stepmother told me that my dad was extremely proud of me and loved me dearly. To this day I often wonder why he never told me these things when I was growing up. It would have meant so much to me to hear those words from him.

I managed to stay single until the early 1980s, when I married a serviceman. We were married for 16 years and, during that time, there was no physical abuse and no children were conceived. Then in 1998 he came home and announced that he didn't love me anymore, and he filed for divorce. Husband number three left me with absolutely nothing. I couldn't even drive because I had never learned how, and even if I could, I didn't have a car. Shortly after the divorce my biological mom died, my daughter nearly died, and I was suicidal. I was an emotional wreck, still longing for love and acceptance.

At the urging of one of my children, I moved to a different state and it was there that God began leading me on a path of discovery. I went to work for a Christian businessman and learned that my supervisor was also a Christian. I was invited to a Bible study they led and then to a Bible-believing church. It was there that I accepted Christ as my Savior, and since then I have seen God perform one miracle after another in my life. I have been provided with a good job, a dependable car, Christian friends who love me, and, best of all, God is healing and restoring me in ways I never thought possible. Counseling over the last few years has helped me understand the lies I believed about myself and my self-worth. The journey has been terribly painful, but I'm glad I never completely gave up. God has filled the void in my life and given me a reason for living again. Bless His holy name.

Testimony Three: Meet Jeanne...

"I began to feel like a failure and to believe that his unhappiness was my fault. If only I were a better wife, maybe he'd be happier."

I married at age 19. Looking back, I remember that Bob was in such a hurry to get married. He was attentive to my every need, and he was totally enamored with me. I loved having that kind of attention, and Bob seemed like the perfect guy to marry. We married after dating for just nine months, and for the next several years I was happy. Almost from the beginning Bob wanted me totally dependent on him, and at first I didn't really mind.

After three-and-a-half years our first child was born and I became a stay-at-home mom. Bob became more controlling and didn't like the idea that I was maturing. Five years into our marriage I delivered our second child. I had severe complications during the birth, and while I was in the hospital recovering, Bob came into my room and told me how embarrassed he was at the way I behaved while I was in labor. Our relationship began to deteriorate rapidly, and Bob became even more controlling and aggressive toward me.

When I saw how disgusted Bob was with me, I began to feel like I couldn't do anything right for him, including having his child. I began to feel like a failure and to believe that his unhappiness was my fault. If only I were a better wife, maybe he'd be happier.

His power and control over me actually increased because I unknowingly helped him become this way. I routinely described him to others the way I wanted him to be, not the way he really was. I constantly covered up his failings and described him as a near-perfect husband. I created a false illusion of a perfect couple to those in our church as well as to our families. I thought it was my job to build him up in front of others. Little did I know that I would pay a high price later on for painting the wrong picture.

There was a lot of sexual abuse and intimidation in our marriage. Bob constantly lied to me in an effort to keep me off balance and create uncertainty in my life. He had me convinced that I was always wrong, so I regularly apologized for everything. During the seventh year of our marriage I sought out a Christian counselor to see if he could help me become a better wife to my husband. I was a Christian, and I wanted to be obedient and submissive to him like the Bible says.

Bob and I were both very active in our church, and I was involved in music and teaching. We were in a Bible study together, and we were a rather high-profile couple in our congregation. When I told Bob I had seen a counselor, he became very upset and told me that I didn't need a counselor.

I continued to see the counselor, and after about three months I developed enough trust in him to disclose the forced sex that Bob had subjected me to. For the first time, I actually heard someone call it abuse, and I was told that I didn't have to tolerate it anymore. The counselor advised me that, for my own safety, I should think about separating until I could be sure I was safe with Bob. But as a Christian, I felt divorce was not an option, so I quit going to counseling.

Bob's behavior became much worse. He would smash things in the house when I wasn't home, and he often told me that having an affair might improve my self-esteem. He constantly accused me of being unfaithful to him. I was terrified and had great difficulty sleeping. When I did fall asleep, he would come in, scream at me to wake up, and accuse me of ignoring him and of sleeping around on him.

I couldn't stand it anymore. I finally went back to see my counselor without Bob knowing it, but he spotted me coming out of the counselor's office and became furious with me for going behind his back. I got down on my knees and begged him to go with me to counseling and to give his heart back to God—but he refused. After wrestling with God over the issue of divorce, I eventually reached a point where I had peace about it and decided to end the marriage.

I went to my pastor and tried to communicate to him my fear and confusion. I told him that I was scared of my husband because of his constant anger. To my surprise, the pastor never asked for, or wanted, an explanation. I told other friends in the church about the abuse, and their response was, "Be more submissive," and, "Examine your own heart." Bob agreed to go with me to see our pastor. Pastor asked him, "What is your wife really like?" His response was, "In public she is very outgoing, but at home she's very quiet." I was quiet at home because I was scared to death of my husband!

I met with my pastor alone and told him that Bob had made it clear to me that he was capable of hurting me very badly, and I also told him about the sexual assaults that had taken place. The pastor didn't have too much to say when I finished telling him about the hellish existence I was living.

I finally took our two children and $60 in cash, and we ended up in a women's shelter. Bob cleaned out all of our accounts so I couldn't get my hands on any money. While I was at the shelter, I filed for the divorce and started getting educated about what abuse really was. The more knowledge I acquired, the stronger I became. I confronted Bob about the abuse—he was furious and denied everything. He blamed me for all our problems and ordered me back home at once. He said, "You belong to me and if you don't come back, I'll destroy you." In the months to come, he nearly succeeded at ruining my life.

When it came time to go to court for the divorce proceedings, Bob and his attorney used my faith in God against me to get custody of the children, who were now ages four and six. He brought my daily devotional diary to court, and his attorney succeeded in getting it admitted as evidence. I was questioned and ridiculed about my interpretation of Scripture because I had written in my devotional that I was battling Satan for my marriage. I had printed material relating to my music ministry, and the Scripture verses I had cited were also used against me. I was asked if I thought that I was the Bride of Christ.

My attorney was not a Christian, but I told him that we would tell the truth even if it meant that Bob would get custody of the kids, that I believed God would protect the children if I lost them. Bob's attorney portrayed me as unstable because I had sought counseling. Because of my faith and beliefs, Bob was awarded sole custody of the children.

But God, in His infinite mercy, caused the judge to issue a very strange ruling. He declared that I was the primary caregiver and that I should take care of the children during the day and that Bob would take the children every night. The kids were nothing but a trophy for him because he didn't want them anyway. As long as he had custody of the kids, he still had control over me. The judge gave me 30 days to prepare the children for their new placement, and during that time there were a great many tears.

I can remember Bob coming to get the kids and having to rip them out of my arms. The children would call me at night and beg me to come and get them, but I couldn't. I could hear them crying for their mama as the phone was hung up on the other end, and it broke my heart.

By now most in my church had abandoned me because Bob had been awarded custody of the children. Some husbands told their wives not to talk to me because I had initiated the divorce. Everyone knew what a great guy Bob was because I had created the illusion that he was an outstanding husband and father. The judge's ruling confirmed that perception in the minds of the congregation. I was now viewed as the bad person.

My pastor told me to be quiet and say nothing despite the fact that Bob was running around our small town telling people that I was a drug addict and a whore. I was confronted by people I knew and told I was an unfit mother and wife.

I was unable to find any help from a variety of Christian ministries, though one did refer me to a secular legal advocate. I received training in the area of advocacy and started working as a volunteer while I went back to college. Eventually my position became a paid position, and I was assigned to work in the very courtroom of the judge who gave my ex-husband custody of our children. I continued to care for the children by picking them up from school every day, feeding them dinner, and dropping them off at their dad's at 7:00 P.M. Never once did I say a bad word about their father. I wanted the children to see for themselves what kind of a man he really was.

After two-and-a-half years of this arrangement, I had to move to a city about two hours away, so I told Bob that from now on the kids were his to care for 24 hours a day. I informed him that I would visit them every weekend. About two months later I told him that I wanted the kids back. He consented to let them come and live with me if I agreed not to take them to counseling, would not demand any child support, and would allow them to visit him every summer for six weeks.

I agreed to his demands, and the children came home. Oh, what a joy that was for them and me! To this day he has never asked them to visit him in the summer.

Throughout my entire ordeal I never won one single court proceeding, but despite those setbacks God had a plan for the kids and me. I began looking to the highest court of justice in the universe, God, when I could find no justice on earth.

I have achieved justice by helping other women who have been abused, and I have assisted them in winning child custody disputes. I've given expert testimony all over the state to trained police officers, clerks of court, prosecutors, and attorneys in domestic violence issues. I have been appointed by the Attorney General in my state to sit on the Crime Victims' Board.

My children are doing fine. God protected them throughout the entire ordeal, and He has enabled me to forgive everyone who betrayed me and worked against me. The incident stripped me to the very core of my being after losing my home, my husband, my children, my ministry, and my family. But God still sits on the throne of my heart, and He has proven Himself faithful to me. He is restoring, blessing, and providing for me just like He always has. Blessed be the name of the Lord.

Testimony Four: Angela...Alive Today

"Brad was a lot like my father in that he did a lot of screaming and was verbally abusive. I didn't think much of it at the time because I grew up in an environment that was loud and abusive. I thought that was the way everyone settled his or her differences at home."

My name is Angela and I am alive today because of God's grace and protection, which was extended to me during a very painful and dangerous time in my marriage. Without His miraculous intervention and the assistance of a godly Christian husband and wife who came to my assistance, I might not be here to tell you my story.

I grew up in a Midwestern city in a home where my father was a workaholic. It seemed he constantly tried to prove his worth by working all the time. Dad physically abused my mother and was a prolific screamer. I was never beaten, but I was disciplined quite harshly, which sometimes left bruises on my arms from being forcefully grabbed and pushed around. I remember the terrible things he'd say to me, like, "You're worthless," or "You won't amount to anything." Those remarks cut me deeply and affected my sense of self-worth. I can remember sitting at the dinner table, afraid to say a word. I felt as though I couldn't even breathe for fear he'd go off. My dad hated his parents with a passion, and when his mother died he didn't even go to her funeral.

As a teenager I threw myself into raising and training horses because I loved horses and it got me away from the house a lot. I remember times when my dad would show up and pull me out of the middle of a competition right in front of everyone, just to humiliate and embarrass me. One of the most painful memories I have is when I won an award for second place for the outstanding job I did while employed in sales for a nationwide company. I was so proud of my accomplishment that I called my dad to tell him. He said, "Don't call back until you've won first place," and hung up. Dad made me feel that I was never quite good enough to earn his love and affection, and that if I just tried harder I might be able to win his approval. We were raised Presbyterian, and although I believed in God, my relationship with Him was distant. We went to church more out of obligation than anything else.

Going to college was one of the best things I did at the time to improve my struggling sense of self-worth. While I was at college, I met and dated Brad, the man I later married. Brad was a jock, and insanely jealous. He was also a bully who picked on weaker people. When I ran for vice president of the senior class, he threatened to beat up people if they didn't vote for me—but I didn't notice the warning signs.

Brad was physically big and very popular, and I believed he was going to go places. He looked like he had potential, and he made me feel very important when I was around him. We got married when we finished college.

Several years later Brad became very controlling. He constantly degraded my family, and after a while he refused to let me see my parents. At one point he took the car away from me, and on another occasion he hid my luggage to keep me from visiting them. He forbade me even to speak to my family—it was either him or my family. Brad was a lot like my father in that he did a lot of screaming and was verbally abusive. I didn't think much of it at the time because I grew up in an environment that was loud and abusive. I thought that was the way everyone settled his or her differences at home.

Brad grew up in a home with wealthy parents who spoiled him rotten and gave him everything he wanted. He was self-centered, ungrateful, and demanding. When it came time for Brad's father to retire, his father sold Brad the thriving business. He bought his father out but has hated him ever since—Brad felt his father should have given him the business for free. When his father passed away, Brad refused to attend his funeral or let our children attend.

Under Brad's direction the business continued to grow and prosper, and we built an 8,000 square foot home. It was everything I ever dreamed of having and more. But then the verbal abuse became physical abuse—Brad slugged me in the abdomen. He later apologized and the physical abuse stopped for several years. Then it started again, and this time the abuse became more severe and frequent. Most days were filled with mind games, threats, intimidation, and fear. I kept calling the police, but because of Brad's success and our $1,500,000 home in the community, they automatically extended a higher degree of credibility to him than to me. He was able to convince the police that I was the cause of the problems and responsible for the disturbances. Brad was so polite and convincing to the police every time they arrived that he soon had them eating out of his hands. They were so dazzled by who he was and what he owned that they wouldn't listen to me and rarely made out a report unless it somehow benefited Brad. I finally gave up calling the police and suffered in silence.

The violence continued. At one point my husband grabbed me by my ankles and held me upside down over the railing from the third floor hallway, threatening to drop me to my death on the marble floor. I was sure I was going to die. On another occasion I awoke one morning to find Brad holding my dead cat by the tail, swinging him back and forth over my face. My beloved feline had died unexpectedly of unknown causes, so Brad picked him up and brought him in to torment me. Other incidents of abuse included kicking me in the stomach and punching me. Even though we had separate bedrooms, he sexually assaulted me twice and pointed a loaded handgun at me. I can remember one time having a cyst on my ankle that was excruciatingly painful, and Brad knew this. He found me hiding in a closet, dragged me downstairs, threw me on the bed, and grabbed my ankle until I screamed in pain. My screams awakened our daughter, so he finally stopped.

On another occasion Brad broke into my room while I was reading my Bible in bed. He tore all the sheets off the bed and opened the windows to let the freezing air in. Then he sat in a chair for over five hours, just staring at me. Sometimes when I was in the bathroom he would walk up behind me, scream in my ears, grab me by the neck, and shake me. It was apparent that he wanted me out of the house at any cost. A short time I later I found out why—he wanted his girlfriend to move in and take over.

When I refused to get out of my own home, Brad moved his girlfriend in anyway. It took two weeks for my attorney to have her moved out temporarily, but during those two weeks I saw her walking around in our home wearing nothing but a thong and high heels. She slept with my husband in his bedroom, did her laundry in my washer and dryer, and pushed me out of the kitchen. Once while I was making the children their dinner, Brad and his live-in lover came into the kitchen. Brad spit a glob of mucous into the food and said, "From now on we'll cook for the kids." Brad spit on me a number of times during those final months of our marriage.

During the two weeks Brad's girlfriend was in the house, she invited her friends over for parties and had them swim in the pool while I stood by, unable to do anything about it. Brad's powerful attorneys finally had me removed permanently from the house. I was out, and his new love was in.

But God was faithful to me even before I was ordered out of my own home. During the worst part of the abuse, my path crossed with a wonderful Christian woman who was part of the same organization that I belonged to. I was emotionally devastated from the pounding I had been through, and Sue was like a rock I could confide in and lean on. I shared with her what was going on in my life and she committed to pray for me and stand by me. She shared her faith in Christ with me and began to love me like a sister. During that time, Brad told Sue's husband, Brent, that he was going to hire someone to kill me.

Sometime later, after returning from a trip to Texas, I was asleep in my bedroom at approximately 2:00 A.M. when I was awakened by the presence of an unknown man standing at the foot of my bed. I heard him mumble, "I can't go through with this," and then he left. The man was not Brad, and I had never seen him before. Later that morning when I spoke to Sue on the phone, I learned that she had been awakened at 2:00 A.M. by the Holy Spirit and had been prompted to pray for my safety. Sue awakened Brent and said, "I sense Angela is in great danger. We need to pray for her." Both Sue and Brent prayed right then and there for God's protection for me.

Sue and Brent took me into their home and provided me safety, food, and shelter for four months. They stood up for me when my husband continued to threaten me. They escorted me to court and stayed by my side during the divorce proceedings, testified for me, prayed for me daily, and were a constant source of encouragement to me. It was because of their witness that I came to accept Christ as my Savior. It is because of their obedience to God and their willingness to reach out to me that I am alive today.

The abuse has taken a terrible toll on me and I am still hurting badly on an emotional level. I have good days and some that aren't so good, but through it all I have learned to trust in Jesus. I've grown as a person and discovered contentment in the things of God. The healing and forgiving will be a long and sometimes painful process, but I am convinced that God's faithfulness will see me through. One of my favorite passages of Scripture that I clung to during that terrible ordeal is found in Psalm 119:132–134:

> "Turn to me and be gracious to me,
> After Your manner with those who love Your name.
> Establish my footsteps in Your word,
> And do not let any iniquity have dominion over me.
> Redeem me from the oppression of man,
> That I may keep Your precepts."

CHAPTER 11

Ministering to the Abused: Instructions to Pastors and Those Who Counsel

A woman caught in the nightmare of domestic violence and severe verbal abuse has a very difficult time breaking free from the bonds of fear and doubt that enslave her broken heart and tortured mind. Helping her get back on her feet will require a concerted effort by a dedicated and skilled group of supporters and a committed prayer ministry.

Too often the church has been ill equipped and less than enthusiastic about getting involved in the painfully private struggles of its members. As a result, many of God's suffering saints have turned to secular agencies for help instead of to their own faith family. God has something to say about the church's indifference in Ezekiel 34:4:

> "Those who are sickly you have not strengthened, the diseased you have not healed, the broken you have not bound up, the scattered you have not brought back, nor

have you sought for the lost; but with force and with severity you have dominated them."

It's time that every church in America becomes proactive in this area.

If you're going to be light to families in the darkness of this depraved world, don't be caught off guard. You need to be able to provide the support structure each woman needs so she can lovingly hold her husband accountable for his behavior. If we, the church, provide for her physical, financial, emotional, and spiritual needs, her husband cannot hold her hostage to his threats to ruin her or force her back home. She will be able to make wise decisions about her life and relationship, and she will remain strong and confident as God works out the circumstances on her behalf.

The battered woman will need shelter. Is there someone in the church who has an empty apartment or a spare room they can let her use for free? If not, is the church prepared to pay for an apartment until she's back on her feet again? Is that location secure so she will feel safe, and is the landlord trustworthy? Does the woman have a car? If not, how is she going to get around? Is there someone who will loan or give her a car to use? Is her residence on a bus route, or is there someone who can taxi her around?

Does the church have a thrift store so she can find decent clothes for herself and the children? Does the church have a pantry so she can acquire food? What about cooking utensils and toiletries? You will need to provide almost everything she and her children need to survive for weeks or months.

If her husband is on a mission to find his wife and harm her, who will go with the victim to file a restraining order? If you need to call the police, which agency will respond to your call for help? What type of mental health counseling is available for her if she needs it—and where is it? Do you have an attorney in your congregation who will work pro-bono to ensure that if a divorce takes place she will rightfully receive what she is entitled to? Will the same attorney also handle child custody issues that are surely going to arise? If the woman or her children become physically ill and need medical treatment or hospitalization, who will care for them? If she is unemployed, is there anyone in the congregation who will hire and/or train her? Will her children have safe access to education or will Mom have to homeschool them? Does the church have cash in a benevolence fund to handle an emergency like this, or is there a donor you can call on short notice?

Build a bridge to your local women's shelter and draw from their experience and training in this area. You may be amazed at how much the church has in common with these caring crisis workers. They have access to many different programs to help get women plugged into a variety of community resources that will meet the needs I just listed. I believe they will gladly help if you approach them with a proper attitude and ask them to partner with you. I would also suggest that the church take out a liability insurance policy in the event you are sued. It's a small price to pay if things go bad.

Your short-term goal should not be reconciliation, but rather safety for the woman and her children. Be prepared for disappointment, setbacks, and failure. Some women will accept what you are trying to do for them until the storm is over, and then they will go back to the abuser. Two years later you may see the same woman again, worse off than she was before. Others will accept help until they are strong enough to go it alone, and then they will leave the church out of shame and embarrassment. Others may use you by falsely alleging abuse in order to get even with a husband who may have been found to be unfaithful or uncaring. Others will want you to fix all their problems.

Set boundaries as to what you can and will do for the victim. Think with your head as well as your heart. The abused should assume some responsibility for herself as she gets stronger—for instance, job searching, alcohol and drug abuse counseling, returning to school, volunteer work, etc. Insist on regular participation in a small group and weekly counseling.

If the abused will not comply with your safety plan, at some point you may have to give them an ultimatum and let them go. Either they are committed to recovering, or they are not.

Let women minister to women while men play a secondary role from a distance. An abused woman will be more inclined to bond with a woman or husband/wife team than with a man. Do not let a man minister to an abused woman alone under any circumstances. There are a variety of reasons for this.

- If a male counselor is seen by the victim's abuser, the abuser may assume the man is her new boyfriend and harm him in a jealous rage.

- If a man who is assisting the victim is less than honorable, he may attempt to start a relationship with the victim out of pity, sympathy, or a desire to protect her.

- An untrained man can fall victim to the vulnerable woman's desire to be loved, protected, and accepted at any cost. The woman may begin to see him as the only stable influence in her life and believe that she can trust him with all her emotions and desires. There's an old saying, "Those who pray together, lay together." When a man and a woman develop a bond of trust while dealing with some of her most sensitive and painful issues, it is only natural that the next step is going to be some level of physical intimacy. Once that line is crossed, look out—serious consequences will soon follow. As the man continues to exercise bad judgment in this inappropriate relationship, the woman's life and the man's family will be placed in serious jeopardy.

- Placing a battered or abused woman in the hands of an untrained man who ends up becoming romantically involved with the victim could have drastic civil implications. You may find the church being sued for negligent entrustment. If the relationship deteriorates, and it will, the victim is likely to make a claim for all kinds of compensation for being victimized twice.

- If the woman finds herself being rejected by yet another man, she may be willing to make false accusations against him to get even with him. The man may find himself in the police department, defending himself against false criminal allegations that he can't refute.

Let women minister to women. Keep men out of the picture as much as possible unless it is a solid husband/wife team who have had some training or experience in this area. Men should only step into the picture if there is a safety issue for either the victim or the women ministering to her.

If the husband is cooperative and non-threatening, who is ministering to him? The person ministering to the abuser needs to have regular communication with the person ministering to the abused so you can keep the victim informed of his progress or lack of it. This will also help you to gauge his mental and emotional attitude and the timeliness of re-uniting them, if at all.

A battered wife may respond to abuse in many ways. At any given time her emotions may run the gamut from fear, pain, guilt, confusion, love, and anger. She is often terrified, and rightfully so, because she is the one who stands to lose the most in terms of her home, financial security, children, reputation, and emotional and physical well being.

Oftentimes the wife feels powerless to stop the abuse that she has learned to tolerate for so long, and she feels paralyzed and controlled by fear. She may blame herself for the abuse, believing that if she just had done a better job of meeting her husband's demands, he wouldn't have become so violent. It's not uncommon for a battered wife to continue to long for her husband's involvement in her life, if he would just stop beating her.

The wife may still crave her husband's approval and long for his acceptance of her despite his brutality. When the emptiness and pain seem overwhelming, she may begin to hate herself in order to deaden the truth that the man she once loved and gave herself to has used, abused, and rejected her. As she spirals down into the depths of depression, loneliness, and despair, she loses the strength to seek the intervention that her husband needs and deserves, and begins to minimize his sinful behavior.

Some women will display considerable amounts of anger toward their husbands. Does a wife have a right to be angry with an abusive husband? Absolutely. God Himself hates marital violence (Malachi 2:16). The problem is that the righteous anger may deteriorate into a sinful rage that seeks revenge. You know the old saying, "Hell hath no fury like a woman scorned." In my career, I've seen angry women do some very violent things to their husbands. All over the country we have women serving time in prisons because they have killed or severely injured their abusive husbands.

In many cases fear may provoke one of two responses: a passive response or an aggressive response. Passivity is the response that tolerates both verbal and physical abuse and flees from all confrontation, leaving the woman to feel like she is a doormat for her husband to walk on. Passivity prolongs the loss of her own honor and dignity and encourages the abuse to continue. The woman's passivity facilitates the abuser's continued sinful behavior.

An aggressive response by an abused wife results from her desire to get even with her husband for the way he has treated her. Her response might range from withholding sex to never being home to public embarrassment of her husband or to running him heavily into debt. Her aggressiveness may also take on the form of violent behavior, such as killing him, burning down the house, or poisoning his prize hunting dogs. Don't forget what Lorena Bobbitt did to her husband. Ouch! The concept of "How can I love my husband?" is the farthest thing from her mind and heart. But despite the hurt that a woman has endured, she is not to seek revenge.

> "And while being reviled, He did not revile in return; while suffering, He uttered no threats, but kept entrusting Himself to Him who judges righteously."
> —1 Peter 2:23

Each woman must decide at some point in her journey out of domestic violence whether or not she will trust her life and circumstances to herself or to God. God's way doesn't promise instant relief, but He promises to give grace and strength and to work all things together for good to those who trust Him. King David acknowledged his dependence on God in Psalm 23. Think about these comforting promises for a moment, and claim them for yourself.

"The LORD is my shepherd,
I shall not want.
He makes me lie down in green pastures;
He leads me beside quiet waters.
He restores my soul;
He guides me in the paths of righteousness
For His name's sake.
Even though I walk through the valley of the shadow of
    death,
I fear no evil, for You are with me;
Your rod and Your staff, they comfort me.
You prepare a table for me in the presence of my enemies;
You have anointed my head with oil;
My cup overflows.
Surely goodness and lovingkindness will follow me all
    the days of my life,
And I will dwell in the house of the LORD forever."

Choosing a godly response requires that you learn to trust God one step at a time. Remember, Jesus has walked in your shoes and is intimately aware of your pain and suffering. Nothing escapes His watchful eye. A godly woman learns to walk in a way that enables the heart of God to be revealed through her to her husband. She lovingly challenges her husband from a position of safety and strength to surrender his sinful heart and mind to God.

A godly woman is not controlled by fear even though she is rightfully afraid of her husband's continued abuse and threats. She remains steadfast in her dependence on God to supply all her needs and to deal with her husband as He sees fit. She becomes shrewd in all her dealings while remaining innocent of all wrongdoing toward her abusive husband. She exposes her husband for the abusive controlling bully he is. By doing so, she becomes stronger and breaks free from her fear as she invites him to come and know the goodness of God and repent of his wickedness.

When one woman's church refused to believe that her husband was a screaming, threatening bully, she secretly videotaped his behavior and showed it to the pastor and elders. Guess what? The husband was exposed for the fraud he was, and he broke down, admitted he was an angry, controlling man, and submitted to church discipline.

Other women have confronted their husbands and respectfully told them that if they didn't stop the abuse they would call the police and have them arrested and jailed, file for divorce, or get a restraining order to prevent them from coming back to the house. Those are all legitimate ways a woman can lovingly hold her husband accountable while inviting him to repent. A woman who refuses to confront her husband's abusive behavior in order to protect his reputation becomes an enabler for his sinful behavior.

The Attitude of the Church

Now that we have spent some time examining the practical needs of a domestic violence victim, let's look at the position the church should take in these matters. God is in the business of restoring, healing, and forgiving. He is the God of fresh starts and new beginnings, and He loves the abuser just as much as the abused, but the woman's safety comes first.

After 14 years of unrelenting physical abuse, some that was savage, Sandy finally did something about it. She went to her pastor and told him that she was leaving her husband, and then she did. Six weeks later she was back home with her abusive husband. She had succumbed to pressure, mainly from her pastor. By laying all kinds of guilt on her, the pastor persuaded her to return to a man who beat her like a punching bag for most of her adult life. The pastor told Sandy that her marriage was too valuable to end and that her husband had changed in the last six weeks since he had begun counseling him. "Sandy, won't you give him another chance?" the pastor asked. "All you have to do is be more loving, quiet, and gentle. Don't you know the stress he's under? Just keep the kids under control and don't provoke him—everything will be just fine." Sandy returned to her abusive husband out of guilt and fear, and the pastor was able to claim another easy victory. He had saved another marriage.

The pastor sent the woman back to be abused again based on two misleading beliefs: first concerns the sanctity of marriage, and second, the importance of submission in a healthy marriage. From the time the pastor learned of the beatings, his number one goal was to save the marriage. It appears that his sole objective in counseling the woman was reconciliation with her husband. That was mistake number one. Reconciliation is very important, but the woman's safety is paramount.

The pastor should have believed the woman when she told him that her husband had been beating her for 14 years, and he should not have believed the husband when he said he was a changed man. Believing the manipulative and deceptive husband was the pastor's second mistake.

How can a man who beats his wife for 14 years change in six weeks? God is capable of transforming hardened hearts in an instant if He wants to, but this husband was a professing Christian all the while he was abusing her. The only time he ever considered changing was when his wife finally found the courage to get up and get out. A chronic abuser must prove over time, lots of time, that he is a changed man. Some churches believe he's a new creature in Christ and immediately insist that his wife go back because it's her Christian duty to remain married. The women usually return because they are jobless, financially strapped, and have no support system to sustain them until they can grow strong again.

The second reason the pastor mistreated Sandy lies in his misplaced emphasis on submission in marriage. The Christian community believes that in a healthy Christ-centered marriage, it's the husband's job to love his wife and the wife's job to submit to her husband, based on Ephesians 5. It makes a false distinction between love and submission. In fact they are one and the same. What gets lost among the themes of love, submission, and Christ's loving sacrificial relationship to the church is the mutual obligation to submit to one another. That's right—men are required to submit to their wives.

"And be subject to one another in the fear of Christ. Wives, be subject to your own husbands, as to the Lord. For the husband is the head of the wife, as Christ also is the head of the church, He Himself being the Savior of the body. But as the church is subject to Christ, so also wives ought to be to their husbands in everything. Husbands, love your wives, just as Christ also loved the church and gave Himself up for her, so that He might sanctify her, having cleansed her by the washing of water with the word, that He might present to Himself the church in all her glory, having no spot or wrinkle or any such thing; but that she would be holy and blameless. So husbands ought also to love their own wives as their own bodies. He who loves his own wife loves himself; for no one ever hated his own flesh, but nourishes and cherishes it, just as Christ also does the church, because we are members of His body."

—Ephesians 5:21–30

Paul's direction to husbands and wives flows from his encouragement to live a spirit-filled life together as husband and wife, as seen in Ephesians 5:19–21:

"Speaking to one another in psalms and hymns and spiritual songs, singing and making melody with your heart to the Lord; always giving thanks for all things in the name of our Lord Jesus Christ to God, even the Father; and be subject to one another in the fear of Christ."

Paul tells husbands and wives to love and submit to one another. It should be obvious that this passage does not relieve a husband of the need to submit to his wife as well. Nor does the very direct message to husbands to love their wives relieve wives of the obligation of loving their husbands—nor does it mean that loving their husbands comes automatically.

In Titus 2, Paul tells older women to train the younger women to love their husbands—a useless Scripture if loving a husband came automatically. Loving and submitting are mutual obligations in a Christian marriage. Each person is a reflection of the other.

In 1 Corinthians 13, Paul erases any doubt about a husband's responsibility to love his wife: love is present only when men treat their wives with profound respect. Love is not rude, it is not self-seeking, it is not easily angered, it keeps no record of wrongs. Love never injures or controls, and it always protects and nourishes. Anyone who thinks that such love does not call for submission has never tried it. He has never loved his wife the way God intends.

Whatever happened to Sandy? She's dead. She came home one night and her husband killed her in a blind rage. I also forgot to tell you, Sandy's husband was a pastor and is presently receiving extensive psychiatric counseling for his long repressed anger problem while he serves time in prison for murder.

If you have determined that now is the time to take action, do so with a heart desiring God's best for your abusive husband. Responding to his sinful behavior from a position of safety while surrounded by caring people will enable you to rest in God's promise to never leave you nor forsake you.

Finding a safe place to wait on the Lord may be the green pastures where He wants you to lie down and rest until circumstances change. Remember how Jesus responded to the people who beat, falsely accused, and abused him? He trusted the Father, just like you will need to do. God will determine how long, how wide, and how deep your valley will be—and when the time is just right, He will lead you out of the valley experience and restore whatever you may have lost.

CHAPTER 12

The Role and Responsibility of the Church in Ministering to the Abuser

In 1996 I came back from a men's conference with a very large group of men from the church I belonged to at that time. The general theme of the conference was "Becoming a Man of Integrity." One of the men in our group, Kevin, had a wife and seven children waiting for him when he returned home. I thought Kevin was a great Christian husband and father to have seven children. The kids and his wife looked happy and were all well dressed whenever I saw them at Sunday morning services. Several days after returning from the conference, Kevin walked out on his wife and kids, leaving them with no money, no food, and no dad.

Kevin's wife, Phyllis, called me in desperation because she knew I was a police officer and involved in men's ministry in our church. Kevin had threatened her with physical violence, and she was terrified of what was going to happen to her and the seven kids with no food, money, or shelter. Phyllis told me that Kevin had been a control freak for years and had forced her to wear only clothes that he approved of. He had also refused to let her hang any pictures in the house or do any decorating of any kind. He even went so far as to remove the doors from the closets to make sure that she never hid anything from him. Kevin constantly monitored every movement that Phyllis made and accused her of seeing other men, when in fact this mother of seven had been completely faithful. Kevin controlled every aspect of the family's finances and had checking and savings accounts in his name only. The picture that Phyllis painted was drastically different from the Kevin I knew from Sunday mornings. Yet, based on my training and experience, I knew she was telling me the truth.

Phyllis and the children moved into a women's shelter because she had nowhere else to go. The following Sunday, Phyllis and the children showed up for church, just as they did every week, and sat down right where they always did. To my amazement, Kevin was sitting on the other side of the church, staring at her. I couldn't believe it. This man had just abandoned his wife and seven children one week earlier, and then had the unmitigated gall to show up in church to harass her. It was more than I could bear, so I got up and walked over to a friend of mine who was a former college football player and also was involved in men's ministry. I asked him to come with me, and I told him why.

There was no way I was going to stand by and watch this husband psychologically harass his wife in church and get away with it. So we walked right over to him while the service was in progress and asked Kevin to come with us. We walked out the front doors and around to the back of the building, went into an interior office, and closed the doors. Kevin was a very big man at 6'2" and 250 pounds. My friend and I got in Kevin's face and told him that we knew what he had done to his family, and in so many words we told him he was a bum for doing it. We also told him that we had made a pact with one another and the church to provide his wife and kids with food, shelter, and legal help to get her through the mess. We told him that he was not welcome in church on Sunday any more, and then we told him to leave.

Kevin wasn't used to people standing up to him, so he became very angry and told us his marriage problems were none of our business. His bravado meant nothing to my friend, the football player, or to me, the veteran cop. Without my saying it, Kevin knew I was prepared to arrest him right then and there if he started a problem, so out the door he went. During the next seven days I called and asked the pastors to officially notify Kevin not to return to church so that his wife would not have to be subjected to Kevin's tactics again. But to my surprise and disappointment, they would not. Their position was that if Kevin wasn't coming to church, they would not be able to reach him. When I asked the church to contact Kevin, they refused.

During the week I received numerous calls from Phyllis, who said that Kevin was turning up the heat with lots of threats to retaliate. Phyllis was struggling emotionally and beginning to believe that if she just prayed harder and submitted more completely to Kevin, he would change and take her and the children back again. I told her to stay where she was and not to go back under any circumstances unless and until Kevin agreed to counseling and several other conditions. I pledged to stand by Phyllis even if the church refused to do what was right.

The following Sunday Phyllis and the children came to church again and, like clockwork, Kevin showed up also. He sat across from his family, glaring at them while his poor wife did all she could to keep from breaking down. You could see how scared the children were, and by now most of the church knew what was going on.

The congregation was expecting someone in church leadership to step up to the plate and have an usher remove him, but they didn't. My buddy, the football player, and I got up from our seats again, walked over to Kevin, and told him to come with us. We went back to the same room where we had met the first time, restated our unswerving commitment to his wife and kids, and turned up the heat a couple of notches. It's a good thing an outsider didn't walk into that meeting, because it certainly didn't look, sound, or feel like anything you would normally experience in a church. It got downright ugly, and for a few minutes I thought we were going to have a knock-down, drag-out brawl. But we refused to back down, and once again Kevin was sent packing with instructions not to come back until he got his act together. In the occupation I'm in, having people dislike me is nothing new. At that point I was more concerned about the rights of Phyllis than I was about being liked by her husband.

To my surprise, about one week later I learned that Kevin consented to come in for counseling. When he found out that two Christian brothers were not afraid of him and were committed to doing the right thing for his wife, he finally realized that she was not alone in her bid for survival. Knowing that two Christian men were ready to go to war with him, expose him if need be, and protect and help his wife and children unnerved Kevin. That was too much for him to bear, and he finally caved in. As a result of our efforts, Kevin and Phyllis received the counseling they needed and are still married to this day. In fact, they had their eighth child about one year later. They bought a different home, changed churches, and today Kevin still won't talk to me—but that's okay.

The church in America must understand that they have a biblical mandate to care for the poor, the hungry, the homeless, widows, and orphans. They also have a moral and biblical obligation to confront abusers within the church. Hebrews 13:4 says, "Marriage is to be held in honor among all, and the marriage bed is to be undefiled." Beating, controlling, or sexually assaulting your wife is not honoring to a marriage—it's dishonorable. Abuse of this sort is sin, and sin needs to be exposed. When was the last time you heard your pastor give a direct, no-holds-barred sermon to the men in the church about verbal and physical abuse of their wives? Warm fuzzy sermons are not enough. Pastors need to teach men how to love and respect their wives on a regular basis.

Men should be told that domestic violence is a crime against God and humanity, that a man or woman who resorts to violence is guilty, and that the spouse is innocent of complicity (contradicting those who say or imply, "You must have done something to deserve it."). The sermon should include practical information, such as how to recognize signs of abuse and how to encourage a victim to seek help. Hearing this from a respected member of the clergy will give encouragement to friends and family members to step forward and help the victim.

In order for pastors to do this, they will need to become better informed. They should visit women's shelters as frequently as they make hospital visits or house calls. Pastors must remind men that they also need to submit to their wives. Men need to hear from their pastor that their spouse is not their property to use and abuse at will. Straight talk by pastors is needed from the pulpit. There are a lot of men who would benefit from some serious squirming in their pews on Sunday morning because of the neglect and abuse they heap upon their spouses in private while projecting themselves as godly men at church.

But abusers also need to hear that God loves them, is aware of the internal struggles they have, and offers reconciliation and healing for every abuser who is willing to surrender his heart and marriage to God's tender care. God is able to calm the raging storms in the soul of every man who is willing to let Him take control. When presented accurately, it is God's message of love that will melt the heart of an abuser, not a message of condemnation. Remember that the abuser has probably grown up under the hand of an abusive parent and may already perceive God the same way he perceived his father—as angry, uncaring, and judgmental.

Pastors on Overload

Pastors in every congregation in America are already on overload try-ing to meet the routine spiritual and relational needs of their flocks. The demands of officiating at weddings/ funerals/ baptisms, hospital visits, budget meetings, pre-marital counseling, administrative meetings and responsibilities, preparation of sermons, building relationships, etc., take a high toll on pastors and their families. Most pastors have received training in counseling and regularly do it on a short term basis, dealing with issues of rebellious kids, church doctrine, marriage communica-tion problems, and routine people problems. Some are far more skilled than others, depending on their level of education, life experience, and natural giftedness. Many pastors and lay counselors have the skills to help a *verbal* abuser understand his need to change, how to make those changes, and what the consequences will be if he doesn't.

However, I do not recommend that a pastor get involved in trying to single-handedly counsel a violent abuser for the following reasons:

- The complexity of what ails the abuser is often very great and will require significant time and skill to work through his issues. If the abuser has received counseling in the past from the pastor and is still abusing, it's time to refer him to a Christian psychologist or a psychotherapist who specializes in these types of issues.

- Some abusers have a criminal mind, criminal history, a known pattern of violence, drug and alcohol addictions, varying degrees of mental illness, or emotional instability. Few pastors have the time or skill to counsel with men like this. Not all abusers are criminals or have a criminal history, but all of them have significant anger, fear, and communication problems.

- The abuser will likely try to manipulate his wife by relaying messages to her through the pastor if she is in hiding or is protected by a restraining order. If the pastor refuses to cooperate, look out—the stakes just got higher.

- If the abuser decides he isn't getting anywhere with the pastor and begins to believe his wife may not come back to him, the pastor may become the object of his wrath.

- If the abuser feels that he is being treated as an outsider by the church and is kept at arm's length, he may return on a Sunday morning and initiate a violent confrontation in church.

- If the husband has abused his wife because of her religious beliefs or because she belongs to a church he doesn't approve of, then the pastor should be very careful in considering counseling with this person at all.

Very few abusive men will agree to counseling or submit to a reconciliation plan. Still others, knowing that many churches believe in instant conversions, will wait until the opportune time and announce, "I've found Jesus." The pastor may begin to extend to the abuser undeserved credibility, believing that the abuser has significantly changed because of his conversion.

Believing this, the pastor will begin to apply pressure to the wife to meet her husband "halfway" and come back home. Eventually, if the wife doesn't respond submissively to the pastor's pressure, she will undergo a role reversal and be viewed as the sinner responsible for not cooperating with his plan. A violent abuser who attends two or three counseling sessions is not in therapy. He needs to have one on-one counseling with a qualified mental health professional over an extended period of time. This is in addition to spending time in a group with other abusers. Even then, therapy is successful in only 30% of cases.

If your church is going to minister to an abuser who claims he's a Christian, then you need to know that, by ministering to him, you're going to pay a price in terms of time, money, and emotion. This is a ministry that should be entrusted only to mature, levelheaded men who have the time, skill, and fortitude to stay the course. Untrained laypeople should never work in this ministry, and those who are trained should be subject to regular oversight by an elder or pastor.

There is potential physical danger any time you start to pull an abuse victim away from her abuser, because the abuser knows that if his victim gets well, she's going to expose him for the fraud he really is. The abuser fears the prospect of losing his punching bag and having to live alone. He may also resent the prospect of having to pay alimony and child support and, therefore, will take his wrath out on you or your church. At the very least, he will try to manipulate you the same way he manipulated his wife through lying and deception. Be on guard—it's likely to happen. Most abusers have a criminal mind and heart, and they are not above using God and the church to regain control of their wife. The closer you get to his pain, the more uncomfortable he is going to get. The more uncomfortable he gets, the more dangerous he may become.

The spiritual, emotional, and psychological needs of the abuser may be long term, depending on a variety of circumstances and factors. The potential for burnout among your lay ministry people is a real possibility, and you must watch for it at all times.

An ideal ministry team would consist of a pastor, two middle-aged men who are willing to make a long-term commitment to the abuser, and a psychologist or licensed counselor, all within the context of a small group. Depending on the circumstances, the need can range from 90 days to one year, or longer.

What my football buddy and I did to Kevin is exactly what every church in America needs to be doing to an abuser. He should not be allowed to attend the same church as his wife until further notice. The pastor should ask the violent abuser to come to his office during the week at a time when the abuser's wife is not there. Once he arrives for the meeting, have at least two elders or pastors present. Tell the abuser...

- that you are concerned for him and want to help in any way possible to bring about reconciliation, but not on his terms
- that you are prepared to report him to the police immediately if he continues the verbal abuse, mind games, control tactics, and intimidation
- that you view his wife's statements as truthful and are committed to her
- that you may need to refer him to a qualified health care professional for treatment and will agree to visit with him concerning his spiritual life while working in tandem with the health care provider

Let him know that if he wants to restore his marriage, he will have to submit to a reconciliation plan that includes counseling, small group involvement, mentoring with an older Christian man or husband/wife team, and possible psychological testing and treatment if deemed appropriate.

If he has physically assaulted his wife and she has not called the police, call the police on her behalf and report him. The police will interview his wife and, if there is enough probable cause, they will arrest him. Jail is a good place for abusers. He needs to hear in easy-to-understand terms that he has no right to control, terrorize, or abuse his wife. Let him feel what it's like to live in fear while he's locked up. I've seen jail do wonders for a lot of controlling men who were released after a couple of days of being locked up in a 6'x 8' cell. But don't abandon him if he is placed in jail. That may be the very best time to visit him and show your concern by letting him know that God wants to have a personal relationship with him and that your church is willing to be a part of that process.

The abuser needs to hear that his behavior is sinful and is a crime against Almighty God and the church. If the physical abuser is a pastor, elder, deacon, choir director, or the head of a ministry, order him to step down immediately until he has complied with the program and his marriage is restored. Tell him that he is not to attempt to move back into the house with his wife until he has satisfactorily completed counseling and his wife agrees to it. That may take up to a year or even longer, depending on how motivated he is to change and how badly he has abused his wife. It also depends on whether or not his wife wants him back at all. I do not believe the church has the right or the spiritual authority to try and pressure, coerce, or convince a battered woman to go back to her abuser. You may be sending her back to her death! Whether or not to reconcile is a decision she will have to come to terms with on her own within the context of her relationship with God. Any woman who belongs to a church that's run by a pastor or elders who try to pressure her to go back to an abusive husband or ignores her cries for help should leave that church immediately.

Let the abuser know that he is welcome to come into the church during the week by appointment or by pre-arranged schedule if that is where his counseling or participation in an accountability group requires him to be. He is not to attend service at your church if that is where his wife still attends until such time as his wife feels comfortable with him being there. Make arrangements for the abuser to attend church on the other side of town if need be.

Recently a pastor of a large congregation told me that his church was ministering to the needs of a battered woman. One Sunday morning the pastor gave an invitation for anyone who wanted special prayer to come forward to the altar. The deacons and elders came down to anoint with oil, and the battered woman came forward with her head bowed and waited for someone to pray for her needs. The pastor and elders gathered around her and began praying. At about the same time, her husband, who had been sitting unnoticed in the back corner of the church, walked up behind his wife, put his hands on her shoulders, and said, "Honey, it's going to be okay." The terrified woman screamed at the top of her lungs in front of the whole congregation when she realized that her husband, who had beaten and sexually assaulted her a few days earlier, was now out of jail and touching her once again.

Needless to say, it was very disturbing for everyone in the church to watch the ushers escort the man out and to see the distraught wife being helped to a side room for comfort and support. The husband could have just as easily walked up behind his wife and shot her and the men around her, and then killed himself. The world is full of unstable people. You must get a safety plan in place for your church if you don't have one already.

Look for police officers, social workers, child protection workers, correctional officers, sexual assault advocates, crisis counselors, and women's shelter volunteers who attend your church and have submitted to church leadership. Make sure these people are solidly grounded in the Word of God and are mature Christians. Husband and wife teams would be all right if you can find the right couples and the abuser is compliant. Utilize the strong-willed men from the congregation—men who won't back down and who have the capacity to display godly compassion, tenderness, or toughness as part of a crisis team. Provide training that will enable them to deal with the basic physical, emotional, and spiritual demands of dealing with an abuser and the abused. My biggest complaint with Christian men is that many of them are more concerned about being liked than they are about being right. Don't let anyone into the mix who is a religious zealot, either. The last thing an abuser needs is to be hit over the head with a Bible. The love of

God, and men modeling the love of God to the abuser, may soften his hardened heart as time goes on.

What the abuser needs are a few Christian men who are interested in understanding his emotional needs, unafraid of confronting his bad behavior, able to hold the abuser accountable for his progress or lack of it, and have a willingness to help him get his marriage and life back on track.

Don't get me wrong. The greatest need in the abuser's life, above all else, is a right relationship with God. But first try and build a trusting relationship with the man by modeling godly behavior in front of him. I strongly support men's accountability groups and mentoring programs. While talking over a cup of coffee or breakfast once a week, an older, mature Christian man can make an enormous impact on a younger man who is struggling in his marriage relationship. Sometimes just being a good listener and being able to speak words of comfort and encouragement to a younger man can help significantly.

Many abusers have never felt or heard the love of a father, and all they want is someone to affirm their worth and understand them. Spending time fishing, golfing, bowling, etc., can significantly impact the life of an abuser who may be about to give up and end his life or his wife's.

If the abuser is a man who does not know Christ as Lord and Savior, it is certainly appropriate to invite him to church provided his wife does not attend church there. The small group setting is the correct place for an unsaved abuser to be ministered to by group leaders. You may need to pick him up and bring him with you. Have him sit with you in church and make him feel welcome and wanted by you, the church, and by God. If God has prepared his heart, he will warm to the message of a Savior's love, forgiveness, and restoration. Be prepared for setbacks, disappointments, and heartache—some guys just quit showing up and abandon you just when you think they're back on track.

If you're going to minister to an abuser in tandem with a licensed counselor or a psychologist, you need to know a lot about him, if you don't already. Develop a safety plan for yourself and the church using the following guide:

- If you have a law enforcement officer in your church, ask him/her to check the abuser through local, state, and federal records to see if he is wanted by the law. You don't want to spend time with a felon on the run with a history of violence. If you don't have a police officer in your congregation, call your local police department and ask to have the community police officer assigned to your neighborhood stop and visit you.
- Ask the law enforcement officer for his/her help in this situation under the nexus of congregational safety. There is no reason why that officer should refuse to grant your request. The officer may be personally familiar with the offender and give you even more insight into his behavior and past history.
- Meet with the abuser's wife and find out if the abuser has a history of carrying firearms or concealed weapons. Has he ever been arrested for domestic violence, battery, murder, sexual assault, child abuse, animal abuse, arson, or stalking? Has he ever spent time in prison? When and where? Has he ever threatened to kill the pastor or any other member of the congregation? Is he stalking his wife now by following her to school, work, or church?
- Find out from his wife, to the extent that she is willing to tell you, the length, severity, and type of abuse that he inflicted on her. Having this knowledge will help you determine later if the abuser is lying to you about his abusive behavior. The information will help you determine if the abuser is taking ownership of his deeds and is sincerely repenting for what he did to his wife. It's important for him to come to a point where he is willing to admit that he sexually violated or beat his wife and to admit that he is an angry, controlling man who needs and wants help to change.
- If you are uncomfortable with the abuser and/or feel as though you're in over your head, stop what you're doing and send him away.
- Is he on anti-psychotic medication or anti-depressants?
- Has he ever been institutionalized for mental illness?
- Does he have a job? What does he do for a living?
- Is he drug- or alcohol-addicted?

- Has he ever attempted to commit suicide?
- Has any member of his family committed suicide?
- Is he on probation or parole and, if so, who is his parole agent or case worker?
- Will Probation and Parole assist you?
- Does he belong to a racist organization like the Aryan Nation or a Neo-Nazi group?
- Do you have a panic alarm in the church in case the abuser gets out of hand?
- On Sundays, do you have police officers in church who are equipped to handle a crisis?
- Are your ushers trained what to do if the abuser shows up when he's been ordered not to?
- How will they remove him if he doesn't go peacefully?
- Has he been fired from his job recently?
- Who will escort his wife and children to their car in the parking lot after church events?
- Is the lighting in the parking lot satisfactory?
- Is there a need for a restraining order, and if so, who will apply for it to keep the abuser off church property?

In a day and age of students being gunned down in school, mass shootings in office buildings, and churches being robbed at gunpoint on a Sunday morning, you must have a solid church safety plan in place—not just as it relates to abusers, but for all situations.

If I were a pastor and I was asked to make a decision as to whether or not our church should minister to an abuser during an ongoing incident of family violence, my decision would probably be not to. Some exceptions would be:
- if the offender is a younger male who is a member of the congregation and you have a close relationship with him
- if you feel he will submit to your instruction and is teachable as to the proper way to handle conflict resolution, and he admits he was wrong and says he's sorry

- if his history of abuse is very short and is primarily due to a lack of maturity and communication skills
- if he has not committed an act of sexual violence or used a weapon during the abuse
- if you feel the incident of abuse is totally out of character for him and may have been triggered by other factors such as the loss of a job or death of a loved one
- if his wife was not physically injured during the assault

Keep in mind that once the abuse problem is resolved and the crisis is over, there is a high probability that the affected couple will stop attending the very church that got them through their struggle. The reason is because family violence creates such a sense of shame, even after the abuse has ended and the situation is resolved, that most couples can't get beyond the shame and find it easier to go somewhere else where they are not known.

CHAPTER *13*

Starting Over:
Getting Your Life
Back on Track

Whether you are a recovering victim of domestic abuse who is fortunate enough to see your marriage relationship restored, or you have come to realize that your marriage is over, this chapter will provide you with help in getting your life back on track. Getting back on track or getting on track for the first time is hard work. It won't just happen by itself and is rarely accomplished quickly. The memory and effects of abuse can last for decades, but they can also serve as a gauge of how much progress you've made in the process of forgiving, trusting, and loving again. In order to get your life moving forward, you need to consider a twofold process—steps you can take internally and steps you can take externally. First, let's look at the internal.

Grieving

In order for the healing and restoration to take place, you must grieve. Grief is essential and healthy if you want to feel emotionally well again. To grieve means to assess your losses and admit that you are hurting. Once I heard it said that "You can't heal what you can't feel." Grieving frees us up, allows us to go beyond anger, and helps us to focus outwardly once again. When we have honestly acknowledged our loss and the pain we feel, we can stop blaming others for our circumstances.

In the process of grieving, each person needs to take responsibility for whatever they may have contributed to the problem. If you made some mistakes, admit it, repent before the Lord, and make corrections or amends where possible—then forgive yourself.

That means you acknowledge that you're a sinner, have caused some hurts, and also need forgiveness. The sorrow you feel may take a long time to go away and, if it does, that's okay. Being beaten, betrayed, or sexually abused is bound to leave deep and powerful wounds that no one can understand, other than another abuse victim. The Bible invites us to grieve. It's okay to take a hard look at yourself and mourn over the painful trial you find yourself in. Grieving over the magnitude of your loss is a healthy part of your healing.

> "Blessed are the poor in spirit, for theirs is the kingdom
>   of heaven.
> Blessed are those who mourn, for they shall be
>   comforted."   —Matthew 5:3–4

Forgiving

This is going to be very hard for many abuse victims—it will take time and God's help. You need to come to a point where you can forgive your abuser. Corrie ten Boom was an amazing Christian woman from Holland who was captured in World War II by the Nazis. Corrie and her family were sent to a concentration camp for hiding Jews in their home. Her father died in prison and her sister died in the camp—only Corrie survived. One of the prison guards was particularly cruel to Corrie and her sister, and his cruelty was a contributing factor in her sister's death. In her book, *The Hiding Place*, she tells this story. Several years after the war was over, Corrie was speaking in a church. After the service was over she noticed an old man walking down the aisle toward her. As he got closer, she recognized him as the cruel guard from the camp. God immediately impressed upon Corrie that she needed to forgive him, but she said, "I don't I have the strength to do it, Lord. Please help me." In that very instant God flooded Corrie's heart with forgiveness and compassion for the old man. Corrie learned that he had become a Christian, and she knew that God had forgiven him for the horrible atrocities he committed in the camp.

Ask God to give you the day-by-day strength to forgive as you remember what your abuser did to you. God is faithful and He will enable you to forgive. As the memories come back, and they will come, get in the habit of saying, "God, I forgive that person with my mouth and with my mind. Help me to feel the forgiveness with my heart." I promise you, over time the forgiveness will flow. Forgiving does not mean that you forget the offense that was done to you. Healing requires that you remember. Remembering allows you to lovingly hold your abuser accountable for his/her behavior. To tell yourself that you must forget the incident in order to heal is a lie that will eventually lead you to denying the reality of the event. Mark 11:25 says, "Whenever you stand praying, forgive, if you have anything against anyone, so that your Father who is in heaven will also forgive you your transgressions."

Forgiving is not saying that what your abuser did to you is all right. Forgiving is to release your emotional desire to retaliate against your offender for what he did to you. You let go of those feelings of hatred and revenge. Forgiving means you are willing to let God and/or the authorities deal with the offender. Forgiveness doesn't mean that you try to remove the natural consequences that should follow any act of sinful abuse. It's okay to participate in the process of holding your abuser accountable when the motivation of your heart is for him to change and surrender his heart and mind to God.

Forgiving is absolutely essential to healing. As long as you hold on to bitterness and anger, you remain a victim. Your abuser continues to control you from a distance, and it affects the quality of your life for many years after the incident. Somewhere I read that harboring bitterness is like taking cyanide and waiting on the other person to die—you hurt yourself, not your abuser. Holding on to hatred and bitterness occupies the space in your heart that God wants to fill with peace and joy as part of the process of restoring your soul. Once you have emptied yourself of the sadness, pain, and anger, the filling can begin as you thirst after righteousness.

> "Blessed are those who hunger and thirst for righteousness, for they shall be satisfied."
>
> —Matthew 5:6

Many of us want to forgive too quickly. In some Christian circles, forgiveness is a shallow mental exercise performed to numb the pain we need to feel. We don't want to go through the process because it takes time and requires us to feel and remember in order to heal. By working through the pain, we become more sensitive and compassionate to other hurting people. Character development and personal growth occur more often in painful life experiences than in pleasurable times. Our own testimony of process becomes an encouragement to those who haven't yet healed to the point where we are.

> "Blessed be the God and Father of our Lord Jesus Christ, the Father of mercies and God of all comfort, who comforts us in all our affliction so that we will be able to comfort those who are in any affliction with the comfort with which we ourselves are comforted by God."
>
> —2 Corinthians 1:3–4

Forgiveness is a choice we make to extend "grace" to another through God's Holy Spirit. Forgiveness doesn't happen on its own. It is a conscious decision to let go of feelings and trust the abuser to God's hands. Forgiveness is a long-term process for many people, not a quick emotional experience. Saying, "I forgive you," doesn't excuse the effects of the abuse. It's okay to take time to forgive. Reflecting on the magnitude of your loss is a healthy part of your healing.

Your desire to extend forgiveness must never be conditional on your abuser repenting or apologizing for what he did to you. It makes it much easier when someone comes to us and says, "I'm sorry for the pain I've caused you. Please forgive me." But more than likely, you will never get an admission or an apology from the person who wronged you. You must forgive that person anyway, and when you do, you will find your vitality returning along with an increase in your creativity, energy, and imagination.

If people in your church are telling you that you'd be over it if you just trusted God more, they simply don't understand the depth of your wounds. A broken heart needs to heal from the inside out, and that takes time, the Holy Spirit, and lots of TLC. You may have been angry with God for most or all of your life for the circumstances you found yourself in—you may have blamed God for it. If that's true, release that resentment and blame you feel toward God and then ask Him to forgive you for the anger and disappointment you have held against Him.

Don't confuse reconciliation with forgiveness. Reconciliation means a cessation of hostility. One or both parties have agreed to stop hurting the other. Forgiveness means the victim has let go of resentment.

Releasing

Once you have grieved over your loss and have forgiven your abuser, then my encouragement to you is to emotionally release your abuser to God's control. By reaching a point where you can say to yourself and to God, "I release him to Your hand, Lord, to deal with any way You see fit," you're telling God that you trust Him to bring about justice for you in His time and in His way. I've seen some very proud and powerful people who fell into God's divinely created and unfore-seen circumstances and lost everything they once boasted about hav-ing. I've seen men who used and abused others with impunity, who thought that because of their money or position they were untouch-able, and went down in flames and never recovered. God hates pride, and pride comes before the fall. If your abuser has acted this way, don't despair. God will deal with his pride and anger when the time is right.

If the courts have ruled that your abuser is to make restitution to you, alimony payments, child support, etc., don't release him from his legal responsibility. Consequences always follow sin, and God may very well have used the courts to punish your abuser. Don't deny your abuser the benefits of his tribulation by failing to hold him accountable for complying with a court order.

Restoring

If you have survived the abuse in your life apart from God, and many women do, then who will you look to for the restoration of your heart and soul? Will you seek restoration by immersing yourself in educa-tion, becoming financially independent, undergoing years of secular therapy designed to magically help you release your own healing and restorative powers?

Will you align yourself with other abuse victims and live out your life traveling from one self-help group to the next, looking for affirma-tion and safety? Will you throw yourself into the arms of another abuser in an effort to be loved and accepted at any cost?

Sadly, I have seen many women who survived abuse and years later are still as broken, fearful, and dysfunctional as they were the day they escaped their abuser. Several years ago I watched as a line of abuse survivors walked up to a microphone at a domestic violence rally. Through tremendous pain and tears, each one recalled the abuse from 10, 12, or 15 years ago. As I listened to them, it became clear that each woman still was held emotionally captive to her abuser and had never moved beyond the trauma. They were still living out the abuse over and over again—they were still victims. Not one of the women who came to the microphone that night was able to give a personal testimony of God's healing, grace, and power in her life, or could speak in terms of personal victory, growth, or forgiveness. They were stuck in their grieving, and they never learned how to move beyond it. There was no joy or power in their lives. It was one of the saddest things I've ever seen. All of them looked physically exhausted, emotionally empty, and spiritually starved to death.

God, through the power of His Holy Spirit, is the One who renews us day by day, even in the midst of difficulties. He gives each one a free choice to decide whether or not we will surrender our lives and circumstances to His plan or live out our lives on our own, apart from Him. Like a doctor, God freely offers life-restoring medicine to every sick patient. God allows us the choice to either accept the medicine, even though it may not taste good at times, or to push the spoon away from His outstretched hand, and remain sick.

The renewal of the mind is accomplished with God's Word, the Bible, and you cannot know God intimately unless you spend time in His Word and have accepted Jesus Christ as Lord and Savior. It is in His Word that you come to understand His care and compassion for you. It is in His Word that you discover the enormous eternal value God places on you. It is His Word that is a balm to the soul.

Let's look at a variety of Scripture verses that will help to renew your mind, heart, and soul. Write these Scripture passages down on 3x5 cards and read them everyday as you drink in God's goodness toward you.

Renewing

"And do not be conformed to this world, but be transformed by the renewing of your mind, that you may prove what the will of God is, that which is good and acceptable and perfect."

—Romans 12:2

"He saved us, not on the basis of deeds which we have done in righteousness, but according to His mercy, by the washing of regeneration and renewing by the Holy Spirit."

—Titus 3:5

"Who satisfies your years with good things,
So that your youth is renewed like the eagle."

—Psalm 103:5

"You were tired out by the length of your road,
Yet you did not say, 'It is hopeless.'
You found renewed strength,
Therefore you did not faint."

—Isaiah 57:10

"Therefore we do not lose heart, but though our outer man is decaying, yet our inner man is being renewed day by day."

—2 Corinthians 4:16

"He restores my soul;
He guides me in the paths of righteousness
For His name's sake."

—Psalm 23:3

Resting

"When you lie down, you will not be afraid;
When you lie down, your sleep will be sweet."

—Proverbs 3:24

"He makes me lie down in green pastures;
He leads me beside quiet waters."

—Psalm 23:2

"He gives strength to the weary,
And to him who lacks might He increases power."

—Isaiah 40:29

"For I satisfy the weary ones and refresh everyone who languishes."

—Jeremiah 31:25

"Come to Me, all who are weary and heavy-laden, and I will give you rest. Take my yoke upon you and learn from Me, for I am gentle and humble in heart, and you will find rest for your souls."

—Matthew 11:28–29

Healing

"See now that I, I am He,
And there is no god besides Me;
It is I who put to death and give life.
I have wounded and it is I who heal,
And there is no one who can deliver from My hand."

—Deuteronomy 32:39

"O LORD my God,
I cried to You for help, and You healed me."

—Psalm 30:2

"And He said, 'If you will give earnest heed to the voice of the LORD your God, and do what is right in His sight, and give ear to His commandments, and keep all His statutes, I will put none of the diseases on you which I have put on the Egyptians; for I, the LORD, am your healer.'"

—Exodus 15:26

"And He Himself bore our sins in His body on the cross, so that we might die to sin and live to righteousness; for by His wounds you were healed."

—1 Peter 2:24

External Steps for Change

If you made a decision to get your life on track God's way, then you need to surround yourself with two or three older Christian women who are mature in the faith and are willing to lock arms with you and walk with you out of your hell. I strongly suggest weekly involvement in a women's Bible study and as much social activity with other Christians as time will permit. Do not get in a Bible study with a man and begin meeting in a private location, like his apartment. You might start with a singles group at your church. Many of these groups go bowling, skiing, golfing, out for dinner or a movie, etc. You need social involvement, but with the right people.

If you have been fortunate enough to see an end to the abuse in your marriage and the relationship is now on the mend, I suggest that you and your husband do the following five things right now.

1. If you have had a history of consuming alcohol in your home, get rid of it and don't ever bring it back in your home again. Settling future disagreements with a clear head makes solving problems so much easier.
2. If you and your husband have been hanging around with the bar or casino crowd, get some new friends who are not involved in that lifestyle. 1 Corinthians 15:33— "Do not be deceived: 'Bad company corrupts good morals.'"
3. If you have been doing drugs alone or jointly, get the drugs out and keep them out.
4. If you have been viewing pornography alone or as a husband and wife, get rid of it and never allow it in your home again.
5. Set a date 30 days from now for an accountability meeting with the pastor of your church or with another Christian couple who has a

solid marriage. Knowing in advance that you will both have to account for your behavior and answer questions concerning whether or not you are on track is a good way to stay on track. Then set a date to meet for every 60 days after that for one year.

If you or your husband are not willing to make these changes, you might as well start packing now, because you're not back on track, and in short order your relationship is going to derail once again.

If your abuser was a live-in boyfriend, I have some very tough advice for you. First, having a sexually intimate relationship with your boyfriend is prohibited by God—it is sin. God prohibits sex outside of marriage. Either marry him or get rid of him. My advice is to get rid of him as soon as it's safe to do so. Any man who lives with his girlfriend doesn't love her according to God's standard. Cut off all sex to him and tell him, "No more until we're married." See how long he sticks around. He's simply test-driving to see if he wants to keep you. I guarantee you that as soon as you don't look quite good enough, fail to live up to his expectations, or start to cause him a little discomfort or inconvenience, you're history. Love is a commitment, not a test drive. God will not bless an intimate relationship outside of marriage.

There are also safety considerations. Statistics show there is a significant percentage of child sexual assault and child abuse perpetrated on the children of women who have live-in lovers. While mom is gone to work, the boyfriend may be involving the kids in drugs and alcohol, or having sex with them. The kids see mommy go to bed at night with someone who isn't her husband, and they grow up believing that marriage is not a sacred institution ordained by God. When the children become teenagers, they feel perfectly comfortable getting in bed with a boyfriend or girlfriend because mommy does it, too. How can you tell your children not to engage in sex when you're sleeping with someone who's not your husband?

In summary, if you're single, there are five external changes you should consider making in order to get your life on track:

1. Get your boyfriend out!
2. Get the booze out.
3. Get the drugs out.
4. Get the pornography out.
5. Get God in and keep Him in.

Several years ago there was a study done among domestic violence victims in Memphis, Tennessee. It showed that 40% of domestic violence victims were assaulted by co-habitating boyfriends. Ninety-two per cent of assailants used drugs or alcohol on the day of the assault.

Dating

I suggest you read and follow the godly advice of Dr. Don Raunikar in his book *Choosing God's Best*. Dating is a subject that is far too big to discuss in this book, so I will touch only on dating as it relates to personal safety. Don't ever forget that there are millions of deadbeat men out there who will use you up, empty you out, and throw you away without batting an eye. Here are some guidelines to follow:

- Examine your date and see if any of the character traits I outlined in chapter two apply to him. If they do, don't ignore the warning signs—discontinue seeing him.
- If you're getting serious about the person you're dating, check out your "knight in shining armor" at the courthouse or on the Internet. You may be surprised to find out that he has a violent criminal record for murder or armed robbery, child abuse, or sexual assault. The police or the court may even want him for alimony or child support. Remember, your boyfriend probably isn't going to tell you about a past like that, but if he does, his version of what happened will only be partially true and will include blaming someone else for his troubles. Don't be afraid to play detective and listen to your instincts. He may not have even told you his real name.
- Stay out of the bar scene—it's no place to meet a quality guy. I know that's going to limit your options, but if you're going to trust God with

your life, trust Him with a date. Looking for love in all the wrong places could get you hurt badly.

There is so much more to say on this subject, but perhaps it is best left for another book. I close this final chapter with a word of encourage ment to you. Chances are, the mess you find yourself in took years to get that way. It is probable that your journey out of domestic violence will be long and, at times, painful. Change might come only in tiny increments. But God is faithful, and He will move you onward and upward as He sees fit, just like the women in the testimonies featured in this book. It is my hope that when the process of healing and restoration is over and the "Sunrise from on high" has proven Himself faithful, you will look back in amazement and gratitude and say, "Blessed be the name of the Lord!"

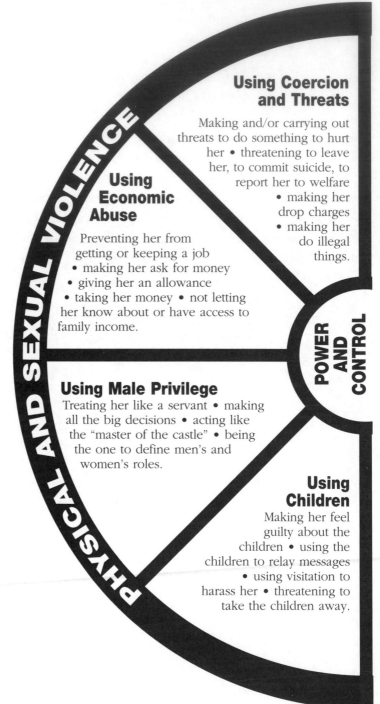

PHYSICAL AND SEXUAL VIOLENCE

Using Coercion and Threats
Making and/or carrying out threats to do something to hurt her • threatening to leave her, to commit suicide, to report her to welfare • making her drop charges • making her do illegal things.

Using Economic Abuse
Preventing her from getting or keeping a job • making her ask for money • giving her an allowance • taking her money • not letting her know about or have access to family income.

POWER AND CONTROL

Using Male Privilege
Treating her like a servant • making all the big decisions • acting like the "master of the castle" • being the one to define men's and women's roles.

Using Children
Making her feel guilty about the children • using the children to relay messages • using visitation to harass her • threatening to take the children away.

Power and Control Wheel

Using Intimidation

Making her afraid by using looks, actions, gestures • smashing things • destroying her property • abusing pets • displaying weapons.

Using Emotional Abuse

Putting her down • making her feel bad about herself • calling her names • making her think she's crazy • playing mind games • humiliating her • making her feel guilty.

POWER AND CONTROL

PHYSICAL AND SEXUAL VIOLENCE

Using Isolation

Controlling what she does, who she sees and talks to, what she reads, where she goes • limiting her outside involvement • using jealousy to justify actions.

Minimizing, Denying and Blaming

Making light of the abuse and not taking her concerns about it seriously • saying the abuse didn't happen • shifting responsibility for abusive behavior • saying she caused it.

Donald Stewart is available
for keynote addresses,
workshops, and conferences.

Send queries to:

Donald Stewart
C/O Midwest Turn-A-Round Trainers
PO Box 11505
Green Bay, WI 54307-1505
midwesttrainers.com

www.newhopepublishers.com

n e w